DATING ADVICE FOR WOMEN

Keep Your Panties on and Choose Love Over Lust

DR. A.M. BENJAMIN

ACKNOWLEDGMENT TO THE READER

Thank you for picking up *Dating Advice for Women: Keep Your Panties on and Choose Love Over Lust*. This book is for every woman who has ever questioned her own pace, wondered if slowing down would cost her a relationship, or felt the sting of giving too much too soon. You chose to read this because you value your heart, your peace, and your power. That decision alone matters.

You will not find judgment here. Your past is not on trial nor a problem to fix. What counts is the clarity and self-respect you build from this point forward. Each chapter offers tools, stories, and straight talk to help you set boundaries, see patterns, and choose partners who treat you with care.

Thank you for trusting me with your time and attention. I hope that these pages help you protect your heart, sharpen your instincts, and date with confidence on your terms, at your pace, with your worth at the center.

FOREWORD

I was both flattered and challenged when asked to write this foreword. I'm an expert only in my own experience. Through many conversations with close girlfriends over the decades, however, I believe my experience is fairly representative of what most of us endure to eventually (if we may be so fortunate) find the partner we choose to spend our lives with. I don't say "suffer through" lightly. While my sister married a wonderful man right out of high school and had 29 solid years of marriage until she passed from cancer, most of us aren't that lucky or fortunate.

My own experience, being single and raising children alone for 20+ years, was far from easy. There were many years I chose not to date or open myself up to a relationship at all because my children were young and I wanted to raise them in peace. I found that impossible with the emotional roller coaster of dating. So, I raised my children alone and in peace for about 15 years. Then, when they were in high school, I felt ready to date again.

What I found in the era of Bumble, Match, and "easy" connections was grown men with a "kid in a candy store" mentality. It felt impossible to meet a quality man, or find someone looking for anything other than easy sex at my (or any woman's) expense. I was ghosted more times than I can count. I was drained, frustrated, humiliated, and often felt defeated. I had to take regular breaks from dating and dating apps to clear my head and restore my self-esteem. Inevitably, after a few months, I felt ready to try again. Then it was back to the roller coaster.

During those difficult years, I read many books and turned to a popular male dating coach's writing, blog, and website. I found reading a man's perspective finally helped me understand where men were coming from and see the dating challenges through a new lens. I stopped taking things personally and learned to evaluate a man's actions (not words) and see whether, over time, his actions matched his words. For this reason, I think "Dating Advice for Women: Keep your panties on" is the most solid dating advice out there now, in 2025. It resonated with me for many reasons.

First, I found the male perspective invaluable because often women just think differently. I know I do. Next, possibly the most important advice you'll ever get (and that I shared with many girlfriends through the years) is to simply wait for a commitment before having sex – ie, "keep your panties on"! This is detailed in Chapter 6. Following this simple yet powerful idea is the biggest takeaway. Other things that resonated with me are:

- Ignore how you feel on a date, assess how you feel the next day. Observe the man's follow-up or lack thereof.
- Look for consistency and communication, rather than "chemistry." In fact, ignore chemistry if you can and keep your head clear.
- Decline last-minute requests and avoid late-night texting. I used to literally turn my phone to "silent" at 9 pm to avoid these traps.

- Red flags will be everywhere without you looking for them, so start focusing on green flags instead - see Chapter 10.

Finally, you may be nodding in agreement… but the hardest part is doing these things and dating differently when it feels so difficult and often hopeless. This is where the practical exercises and worksheets come in. Doing them helped me shift my own perspective and thinking to a more objective way, and not give up on love. I encourage you to give them a try.

In summary, I believe if I could find love (in my 50s, no less!), then surely we all can. It's a matter of patience, perspective, and perseverance. Emphasis on perseverance. I had to remind myself, "there's a lid for every pot," many, many times over the years. This book will give you the guidance and tools to persevere through the minefield of dating in the 2020s with confidence and peace of mind while choosing the pace and the man that's right for you. One final word (Dr. Benjamin's advice in a nutshell), and I learned this for myself: the right man will wait. Trust in that.

- Colette Chalier
September 2025

CONTENTS

INTRODUCTION

You've been here before.

The connection felt strong, the chemistry was intense, and you let things move fast...just too fast. For a while, it felt good. Then came the shift: mixed signals, emotional distance, and silence. And once again, you're left wondering, *was it ever real?*

If you've ever mistaken sexual chemistry for love, ignored red flags because the passion was high, or felt pressured to give in to keep someone's attention, you're not alone. Many of us were taught, directly or indirectly, that physical intimacy could secure emotional commitment. But in reality, rushing into sex often clouds judgment, hides warning signs, and creates a false sense of closeness that fades as soon as the heat cools.

Keeping your panties on isn't about shame or playing games; it's about power. It's about protecting your body, heart, and peace until someone has proven they deserve them. This isn't about playing games, following outdated rules, or making intimacy a bargaining chip, but about taking back control of your pace, your boundaries, and your emotional well-being.

WHO THIS BOOK IS FOR

This book is for you if:

- **You keep getting attached too quickly.** You meet someone, feel an instant spark, and move fast, only to end up confused or hurt when his attention fades.
- **You confuse sex with love.** Physical chemistry feels like proof of connection, yet commitment never follows.
- **You feel pressure to give in.** You worry a man will leave if you slow down or set boundaries.
- **You repeat painful patterns.** Situationships, mixed signals, and one-sided effort seem to show up again and again.
- **You want love without games.** You're done with vague rules, guessing, and manipulation.
- **You're ready to reclaim your power.** You want to protect your body, heart, and peace while dating with confidence.

It doesn't matter if you're twenty-something, freshly single after a long relationship, or dating again after divorce. Your past choices are not on trial here. This book isn't written to shame you or question your history. It's here to empower you with clear tools, real talk, and practical steps so you can date on your terms, set boundaries without apology, and choose partners who respect your pace and your worth.

ABOUT THE AUTHOR

Dr. A. M. Benjamin is an author, educator, and emotional intelligence coach. He holds a Ph.D. in Public Policy and Administration and has spent over fifteen years teaching leadership and emotional intelligence to graduate students and professionals.

He is the author of *The EQ of Dating* and *The Busy Professional's Guide to Emotional Intelligence,* and creator of the **Five Connection Styles** framework, which explains how people bond and communicate in relationships.

Dr. Benjamin's writing is direct and practical. He combines research with real-life insight to help readers set boundaries, build confidence, and create healthy connections, whether in love or at work.

A NOTE ON TONE

This book is not here to shame you, lecture you, or question your past choices. Everyone has their own history and lessons learned. What matters now is how you move forward.

You'll find clear, straightforward guidance written in a warm, conversational voice. No fluff, no judgment, no outdated rules. Each chapter gives practical steps and honest insights to help you protect your heart, set boundaries, and choose partners who value you.

The goal is empowerment. You'll gain tools and confidence to date on your terms and create the love you actually want without second-guessing yourself or giving away your power.

In the chapters ahead, you'll learn how to:

- Tell the difference between charm and genuine interest.
- Slow down and see the truth before you get attached.
- Avoid situationships and men who only want access, and not commitment.
- Break free from cycles of over-giving and overexplaining.
- Heal from the patterns that keep getting you hurt.
- Recognize what emotionally available men actually do and choose them with confidence.

If you've ever been told you're "too much" or feared you'd lose someone by holding back, you'll see why the right man won't pressure you, disappear, or make you guess where you stand. He will respect your pace, your boundaries, and your worth.

HOW TO USE THIS BOOK

This book is a **guide and a workbook**, not just a quick read.

Each chapter gives you:

- **Straight talk and strategy:** clear explanations of how chemistry, boundaries, and emotional patterns work so you can see relationships with fresh eyes.

- **Key takeaways:** a focused insight that captures the heart of the chapter.
- **Interactive assessments:** short questions or exercises that help you apply the lesson to your own life and spot patterns in real time.

READ IN ORDER OR BY NEED

Assessments & Worksheets (Free Download)

You can move through the chapters in sequence or jump to the topic you need most.

The early chapters (1–4) focus on slowing down, spotting red flags, and breaking attachment habits.

The middle chapters (5–9) sharpen your ability to read words versus actions, hold boundaries, and pace your giving.

The final chapters (10–12) help you recognize healthy partners, heal from past relationships, and date with steady confidence.

WORK THE ASSESSMENTS

The assessments are not tests. They're tools for self-awareness.

- **Answer honestly.** There are no right or wrong answers.
- **Write it down.** Use a notebook, the space in the book, or a digital journal. Writing slows your thoughts and reveals patterns you might miss.
- **Review over time.** Revisit key assessments after a few weeks or months to see your own progress.

PAUSE AND PRACTICE

Don't rush. After each chapter, take time to complete the assessment, reflect on the key takeaway, and notice where the lesson shows up in your dating life. Apply one change at a time, whether it's holding a boundary, waiting before intimacy, or noticing how a man handles a slow pace.

SHARE YOUR VOICE

When a chapter gives you a breakthrough, talk about it with a trusted friend or leave a review online.

Even a short review, just a few sentences, helps other women find this book and start protecting their hearts sooner. Your feedback also lets me know which insights resonate most, so I can keep creating tools that matter.

By the time you finish this book, you'll have the clarity, tools, and confidence to date on your terms and never again mistake chemistry for love. Let's begin.

1

SEX ISN'T A SHORTCUT TO LOVE

You'll understand why physical intimacy can't create emotional commitment, and how to stop mistaking sex for a relationship-building tool.

You wanted it to mean something. The way he looked at you, the way his hand lingered on yours, the way the conversation flowed as if you'd known each other for years. It all felt different. You let yourself believe this was more than chemistry. And when you finally slept with him, you hoped, maybe even assumed, that it would bring you closer. You didn't say it out loud, but you carried the quiet expectation that intimacy would move the relationship forward.

For a short while, it seemed like you were right. His attention was steady, the spark undeniable, and the connection felt electric. Then, slowly, the shift came. He took longer to respond. The conversations grew shallow. Plans fell apart with vague excuses. You told yourself he was stressed, busy, or distracted. You clung to the idea that you might be overthinking, but deep down, beneath the justifications, you knew that something had changed.

This is a truth many women face at some point. Sex can feel like it's building love, but often, it only builds the illusion of it. It can deepen attachment on your side without truly changing his intentions. And when the illusion fades, you're left holding the hope you thought you both shared.

1.1 HOW SEX CREATES THE ILLUSION OF CONNECTION

When you sleep with someone, your body isn't just registering physical pleasure. It's launching a chemical chain reaction. Oxytocin, usually called the "bonding hormone," floods your system. This is the same hormone released during childbirth and breastfeeding, because it's designed to build trust and emotional closeness. Your brain reads it as: *You're safe. You belong.*

Here's the problem. Oxytocin doesn't have a moral filter. It doesn't check if he's honest, emotionally available, or aligned with your goals. It simply ties the feeling of safety to whoever you're with in that moment.

This is why sex can make someone feel like "the one" even if you barely know them. What feels like deep emotional intimacy might actually be a biological high layered over reality. For many women, this bonding effect is strong and lasting. For some men, it's weaker, short-lived, or irrelevant to their intentions. That's why you can leave feeling closer, while he acts as if nothing significant happened.

When his behavior doesn't match the closeness you felt, you're left confused and questioning yourself. The truth is, sex can deepen a real connection, but it can also create the illusion of one. If you confuse the chemical rush for compatibility, you risk ignoring red flags and overinvesting before trust is earned.

This is why it pays to keep your panties on until you know his character matches his charm. Slowing down gives you space to see clearly, so you can tell the difference between a genuine emotional connection and a chemical spark that fades.

1.2 WHY LOVE NEEDS TIME TO GROW

Love doesn't appear fully formed. It's built step by step through shared experiences, trust, and consistent behavior. Real love isn't about grand declarations in the first week or intense chemistry in the first night. It's about what happens over weeks, months, and years when the initial spark settles into daily reality.

Sex can create the feeling that you already know someone, but true understanding comes from seeing them through different seasons of life. The truth reveals itself in the unpolished moments, how they treat you when they're stressed, whether they keep their word when it's inconvenient, how kind they are when no one is watching, and whether they make space for your needs as much as their own. These answers don't appear after a few passionate nights. They only come with time, by watching how someone behaves when there's nothing to gain, when circumstances are far from perfect, and when showing up requires real effort.

Patience creates clarity. When you resist rushing into emotional or physical attachment, you give love the space to grow into something strong enough to last. And when you give it that space, you start to see who they truly are, not just who they are when the lights are low.

1.3 THE COST OF LEADING WITH YOUR BODY

If you sleep with a man before you know his character, you hand him benefits he hasn't earned. You give him the rewards of intimacy without requiring proof of reliability, loyalty, or genuine interest. Sex too soon can put your body in the driver's seat and shove your judgment into the back. Chemistry might feel electric, but it's not proof of compatibility, shared values, or long-term potential.

When you skip the "get to know you" stage, you're not just speeding things up; you're changing the entire foundation of the relationship. Instead of growing through conversation, observation, and trust-building, the relationship is built on physical gratification. And here's the danger: your body will start releasing signals that say *this is safe, this is special,* even if the reality is anything but.

Here's what really happens:

- **You stop seeing clearly**: Strong attraction feels good, but it can cloud your judgment. You start making excuses for things that should be dealbreakers like his poor communication, his disappearing acts, his inability to follow through because the sexual connection is blinding you to the truth.
- **You attach without security**: Oxytocin bonds you to him on a biological level, no matter his intentions. You might feel safe with him simply because your brain is responding to the chemical high, not because he's actually earned your trust.
- **You lose leverage**: Before sex, you have the upper hand in setting the pace. After sex, it's harder to slow down or walk

away without feeling like you've already invested too much. You may find yourself settling for crumbs of attention just to keep the physical connection alive.

- **You burn out**: When you pour your energy, time, and body into someone who doesn't meet you halfway, it's not intimacy, but it's depletion. Over time, you can start to feel used, unwanted, or undervalued, which can take a significant toll on your confidence.

This isn't about "playing hard to get." It's about protecting your mental, emotional, and physical well-being. Keep your panties on until his actions consistently match his words over time. Watch how he treats you when sex isn't an option. Does he still show up? Does he still invest effort? Does he respect your boundaries? A man worth your body will prove himself with patience, consistency, and care.

If he leaves because you don't sleep with him, he didn't want a relationship; he wanted access. You don't lose anything when a man like that walks away. In fact, you win by avoiding heartbreak, wasted time, and emotional drain. Your body is not a lure, a bargaining chip, nor is it a shortcut to love. It is the prize, and only a man who has proven his worth over time should get the privilege of claiming it.

Sex changes the dynamics of a relationship, sometimes in ways you don't see until it's too late. The moment you cross that line, you lose the clean view you had of his character because chemistry starts making decisions for you. Keep your panties on long enough to see who he is without the influence of sex, and you'll learn in weeks what could otherwise take months, or heartbreak, to figure out.

How to Spot the Men Who Won't Wait

Some men show their real intentions as soon as sex is taken off the table. They'll either step up and keep investing in you, or they'll vanish, push, or pout. Your job is to watch closely and believe what their behavior tells you.

Signs he won't wait:

- He gets frustrated or sulky when you hold your boundary. Instead of respecting it, he treats it like a hurdle to overcome.
- His compliments shift to your body more than your personality, intelligence, or values.
- He pressures you with "proving" lines like, "If you like me, why not?" or "We're adults, what's the problem?"
- His effort drops when sex isn't happening. There are fewer texts, fewer dates, and less interest in connecting.
- He tries to negotiate your boundaries by suggesting "just a little" or "we don't have to go all the way."
- He skips emotional depth and keeps conversation surface-level because he's not interested in building a bond without physical payoff.

Signs he will wait:

- He respects your pace without guilt-tripping or making you feel like you owe him something.
- He keeps showing up with consistent communication and plans, even when sex isn't on the horizon.
- He invests in getting to know you, your story, your opinions, your life, instead of rushing to get you into bed.

- He supports your boundaries and even appreciates that you value yourself enough to have them.

Bottom line: A man who won't wait is doing you a favor by showing his hand early. When you keep your panties on, you filter out men who want access from men who want you. That's not a loss; it's a shortcut to clarity.

1.4 BREAKING THE "SLEEP TOGETHER FIRST, FIGURE IT OUT LATER" CYCLE

If you've been in the pattern of rushing into intimacy only to feel disappointed or blindsided when interest fades, you need a new approach. Sex too soon can create false closeness, cloud your judgment, and make it harder to see red flags. Flipping the script starts with clear boundaries and consistent observation.

Here's how to change the pattern:

1. **Decide your pace before you meet someone.** Set clear boundaries while you're still thinking clearly, not in the heat of the moment. Know in advance how long you want to wait before becoming physically intimate and commit to that decision. This isn't about following someone else's rule or a set timeline; it's about protecting your clarity so you can truly see the person in front of you before deepening the connection.
2. **Watch for consistency.** Pay attention to actions over time, not just words. Notice if he shows up when it's inconvenient, remembers the details you've shared, and makes space for you in his life without needing to be asked. Consistency before intimacy is the strongest indicator of the consistency you can expect afterward.

3. **Build non-sexual intimacy.** Prioritize activities that create a genuine connection, such as deep conversations, shared hobbies, and experiences that require teamwork. These moments reveal values, communication style, and emotional availability in ways physical attraction alone never can.
4. **Trust what you see, not what you hope.** If he is dismissive, distracted, or unreliable before sex, intimacy will not change that. Build your expectations on evidence you can observe, not on the potential you imagine.

When you lead with your body, you give away your most intimate gift before confirming the other person's intentions and emotional capacity. However, when you lead with your standards, you stay in control of your pace, your boundaries, and your choices. This shifts you from waiting to be chosen into consciously deciding who earns deeper access to you.

Key Insight:

Sex can be beautiful, passionate, and deeply connecting, but it can't substitute for love that's built on trust, time, and shared values. If you want to protect your heart and energy, you have to protect your body first. Love needs space to grow. Give it that space, and you'll never again mistake the rush of attraction for the foundation of a real relationship.

Interactive Assessment:

Pause here and complete the **Sex Isn't a Shortcut to Love Assessment** by scanning the QR code at the beginning of the book.

2

WHY YOU KEEP GETTING HURT

You'll see the patterns that have kept you stuck, so you can break the cycle of quick attachment and repeated heartbreak.

You told yourself it would be different this time. He seemed so into you, the chemistry was instant, and the connection felt real. You let things move quickly, maybe faster than you planned, but it didn't feel wrong in the moment. Then, just like before, the energy shifted. His calls became sporadic, his texts shorter, and his effort thinner. You start wondering if you imagined the closeness. And here you are again, replaying every detail, searching for the turning point, and asking yourself, *why does this keep happening to me?*

If this cycle feels familiar, it's not because you're cursed or destined to fail at love. It's because certain emotional habits, blind spots, and attachment patterns are quietly running the show. You may be ignoring early red flags because the initial rush feels intoxicating. You might be hoping potential will turn into reality if you give enough, forgive enough, or hold on long enough. You could be mistaking chemistry for compatibility, or attraction for alignment.

The truth is, relationships rarely fall apart suddenly. They unravel in small ways that are easy to miss when you're focused on how much you want it to work. But once you learn to see these patterns early, you stop wasting months or years on relationships that were never built to last. The good news is you can break the cycle, but it starts with being willing to see the truth, even when it's uncomfortable.

2.1 HOW RUSHING INTIMACY HIDES RED FLAGS

When you move too fast, the thrill of attraction and the closeness of physical intimacy can distort your judgment. That initial spark can trick you into thinking you know a man well enough to trust him, when in reality you've only seen fragments of who he is. Your body releases feel-good chemicals like oxytocin and dopamine that strengthen attachment and create a false sense of safety. In that haze, it's easy to explain away behavior that doesn't match your long-term needs.

Strong chemistry can blind you to warning signs. You might excuse his inconsistent communication because the in-person spark feels undeniable, downplay a disrespectful comment by telling yourself "he's great most of the time," or mistake physical attraction for emotional depth even though you have not yet seen how he handles stress, conflict, or commitment over time. That early rush acts like a filter, softening red flags into pink ones or making them seem invisible.

The problem is those warning signs don't fade. Instead, they just get harder to see and harder to address once you're emotionally and physically invested. By the time reality hits, you may feel too attached to walk away easily. That's why you keep your panties on until you've seen his consistency without the influence of sex. It's not about playing games but about giving yourself the clarity and control to decide if he's worth the investment before your body's chemistry makes the decision for you.

2.2 FALSE INTIMACY VS. REAL EMOTIONAL BONDING

Sex can make you feel like you've built something deep. You might stay up talking for hours afterward, share personal stories, and think, "I've never connected with someone this fast." But that's not real intimacy; it's false intimacy. It's the closeness created by a flood of hormones and the novelty of attraction, not the grounded trust that grows slowly and steadily over time.

When you lead with sex, you risk mistaking that chemical high for genuine connection. It feels like you've skipped the awkward getting-to-know-you stage, but what you've really skipped is the proof of who this person is when the thrill fades. You haven't seen how he treats you when he's stressed, how he handles disagreements, or whether his words hold up in the real world.

Real emotional bonding is built in the everyday moments when there's nothing to gain but deeper understanding. It's in conversations that go beyond charm and flattery, in actions that quietly match promises, in care that's offered when it's not easy or convenient. It's the slow accumulation of trust, respect, and emotional safety.

If a man's presence in your life shrinks the moment you're not in his bed, you never had intimacy; you had temporary access. And temporary access is not a foundation for lasting love. This is why you keep your panties on until you've seen who he is without the sexual rush clouding the truth. The right man will want to know you, not just have you.

2.3 THE RUSH THAT CLOUDS YOUR JUDGMENT

Early attention can feel like a surge of relief, especially if you have felt overlooked or undervalued. Someone notices you, wants you, and the glow of being chosen can be addictive. That hit of validation can trick you into believing a strong connection exists before you have real evidence.

Sex too soon intensifies the illusion. Oxytocin and dopamine flood your system, creating a chemical bond that feels safe even when the relationship is untested. Your body signals trust while your mind is still gathering facts. The pull to stay and ignore warning signs grows stronger.

This is how a pattern forms:

1. You meet someone and rush into intimacy.
2. The early closeness feels deep and exciting.
3. Over time, inconsistency or disrespect surfaces.
4. You pull back hurt and confused, then repeat the cycle with someone new.

Each round erodes self-confidence. You start to accept less effort, less respect, and smaller gestures of care because you confuse attention with commitment.

Keeping your panties on is not about playing games. It is about giving yourself the chance to observe who he is without the haze of hormones. A man who values you will show patience, respect, and consistent effort when sex is not an option. If he disappears, you have your answer before your heart is entangled.

2.4 BREAKING THE CYCLE FOR GOOD

What keeps you in the loop is not bad judgment; it is speed. Moving fast hides character flaws and magnifies chemistry. When attraction outruns discernment, charm feels like compatibility and attention feels like love.

Slow dating changes the equation. By holding your physical boundary:

- You watch how he handles frustration and delayed gratification.
- You see if his words match his actions over time.
- You test whether his interest survives without instant rewards.

True validation comes from self-respect, not from fleeting affection. Intimacy is a privilege earned through trust, reliability, and shared values. Protect it until someone proves they deserve deeper access to you. The right partner will not pressure you. He will respect the pace that keeps you safe, valued, and certain.

Key Insight:

You keep getting hurt when you move faster than truth can surface. Quick intimacy floods your system with chemicals that feel like connection while hiding the gaps in character, consistency, and real compatibility. Slow down. Hold your boundary. Let time reveal who a man really is before you give him deeper access. Attention is not commitment. Patience protects your heart and gives love the chance to grow on a foundation of respect and proof, and not on hormones and hope.

Interactive Assessment:

Pause here and complete the ***Break the Cycle of Quick Attachment Assessment*** by scanning the QR code at the beginning of the book.

3

THE POWER OF PAUSING

You'll learn how slowing down exposes a man's true intentions and helps you separate charm from genuine character.

Slowing down in dating is not a loss of momentum. It's a strategy that exposes a man's true intentions and separates surface-level charm from genuine character. One of the biggest dating myths is that if you don't "keep things exciting" early on, you'll lose his interest. The truth is, if taking your time makes him disappear, he was never invested in anything real. His exit is not a rejection but a filter that saves you from deeper disappointment.

Pausing isn't about killing the vibe. Instead, it's about creating enough space for the truth to surface. Without rushing into physical intimacy, you can see how he acts when there's no instant access to your body. Does his interest grow when he's required to earn your trust? Does he keep showing up when the focus is on connection rather than gratification?

When you keep your panties on a little longer, you give yourself the gift of clarity. You see patterns, not just promises. You notice how he communicates, how consistent he is, and whether his words match his actions over time. That clarity can save you months, or even years, of pouring into someone who was never aligned with your values or vision for a relationship. The pause is your power. In a dating culture that pushes speed, the women who master patience are the ones who end up with relationships that are steady, respectful, and built to last.

3.1 WHAT SLOWING DOWN REVEALS ABOUT THEM

When intimacy isn't immediately on the table, you give yourself a clear window into who a man really is without the fog of sexual chemistry clouding your judgment. By removing the distraction of rushing into bed, you create room for his true character and intentions to surface. In that space, you get to notice:

1. **His patience.** Does he stick around and keep showing up without pressure, or does his interest fade the moment he realizes you're not rushing things? A man who is serious about building a relationship will never insist on you taking off your panties too soon. He will respect your boundaries, honor the pace you set, and see it as an opportunity to deepen the relationship. Patience is one of the clearest signs of genuine interest because it shows he's not here for a quick win but to build something lasting.
2. **His consistency.** Does his effort remain steady over weeks and months, or does it taper off when physical intimacy isn't immediately available? Consistency is the proof of commitment. If he disappears when there's no quick payoff, you have your answer without having to get hurt in the process.

3. **His communication style.** Can he sustain meaningful, engaging conversations that go beyond flirting and sexual innuendo? Is he genuinely curious about your thoughts, feelings, and experiences? A man who can connect with you emotionally and mentally without relying on physical intimacy is showing that he values the whole of who you are.
4. **His intentions.** Is he truly here to know you, or is his interest transactional, aimed at getting access to your body? Time and patience will reveal whether he's interested in partnership or just looking for short-term gratification.

Slowing down is not about playing games but about protecting your clarity. It's the fastest way to separate a man who's genuinely invested from one who was never planning to stay. By keeping your panties on until you have evidence of his patience, consistency, emotional connection, and genuine intentions, you protect your heart and give yourself the best chance at finding a relationship built on respect, trust, and shared values.

3.2 EMOTIONAL SOBRIETY BEFORE PHYSICAL INTIMACY

Emotional sobriety is your ability to see a person and a situation clearly, without being swept away by feelings, fantasies, or the chemical high that comes with physical intimacy. Think of it like being clearheaded before making a major life decision. You wouldn't sign a contract you haven't read, and you shouldn't give someone intimate access before you've read the "contract" of their character.

Sex changes the emotional chemistry of a connection. When you're physically intimate, your body releases a cocktail of hormones: oxytocin, dopamine, serotonin, that can create a powerful sense of closeness and safety, even if that closeness isn't earned. You might feel like you've known him forever after a single night, or believe the bond is deeper than it is simply because your brain is under the influence of those chemicals. This is why emotional sobriety matters; without it, you can confuse intensity for intimacy and attraction for compatibility.

Pausing before sex allows you to keep your emotional and mental state steady long enough to see the relationship for what it truly is. You get the space to notice patterns, evaluate his consistency, and see how he treats you without the instant reward of physical intimacy. You can ask yourself important questions: Does he invest in knowing me when there's nothing physical on the table? Does he show emotional maturity when we disagree? Does his life align with the kind of relationship I actually want?

The difference between choosing someone with a clear head and falling for someone under the influence of chemistry is massive. One leads to grounded decisions based on trust, respect, and alignment; the other often leads to regret, wondering how you missed the signs that were there all along.

Emotional sobriety is about protecting your ability to make choices that serve your long-term happiness instead of your short-term craving. By keeping your panties on until your mind and heart agree he's earned that level of access, you're choosing to love with clarity, and not chemistry.

3.3 SEPARATING CHEMISTRY FROM CHARACTER

Chemistry can feel like a drug. The spark, the butterflies, the giddy energy that makes you check your phone every few minutes can be intoxicating. That rush can convince you you've found something rare, but chemistry alone isn't proof of relationship potential. You can have incredible chemistry with someone who has no interest in commitment, no capacity for emotional depth, or no alignment with your values.

Character is an entirely different measure, and it only reveals itself over time. You see it in the small, consistent choices a man makes when the excitement wears off:

- Does he keep his word, even when it would be easier not to?
- Does he show respect when things don't go his way, or does he become dismissive, defensive, or manipulative?
- Does he treat others well, waitstaff, strangers, family, when there's nothing in it for him?
- Does he act with integrity even when doing so is inconvenient or costs him something?

These traits can't be measured in the heat of early attraction. They show up in quiet moments, during challenges, and overtime. That's why slowing down is essential. It creates the space to see if the man who gives you butterflies also has the backbone, emotional maturity, and consistency to build something worth keeping.

When you keep your panties on, you give yourself the chance to measure him by his character, not just the high of chemistry. The right man will not only make your heart race, but he'll also make you feel safe, respected, and certain about where you stand. Chemistry can light the match, but character is what keeps the fire burning.

3.4 OBSERVING BEHAVIOR WITHOUT ROSE-COLORED GLASSES

Infatuation has a way of blurring the truth. In the early stages, it's tempting to focus on the qualities you hope are there while downplaying or ignoring signs that something's off. You want him to be the one, so you interpret his actions through a lens of optimism rather than accuracy. The problem is, hope can blind you to patterns, and patterns are where the truth lives.

Pausing shifts you out of fantasy mode and into observation mode. You're no longer rushing to decide how you feel; you're giving yourself the space to watch how he shows up. You're not just listening to his words; you're tracking whether his behavior supports them. Ask yourself:

- **Is his attention steady or sporadic?** Does he make time for you consistently, or only when it suits him?
- **Does he follow through on what he says?** Does his action back his promises, or do they evaporate once the moment passes?
- **Do his actions line up with the values he claims to have?** Anyone can say they value honesty, respect, and loyalty, but does he actually live them?
- **Do you feel calm and respected around him, or anxious and uncertain?** Your body often registers the truth before your mind is ready to face it.

Without the fog of physical intimacy, you can see the whole picture and not just the highlights. You're able to spot inconsistencies, measure his reliability, and decide if his presence brings peace or instability.

Key Insight:

Pausing doesn't push the right man away but filters out the wrong ones. The truly interested man will value the connection you're building and respect the pace you set. The man who disappears because you're not moving fast enough just saved you time, energy, and heartache by showing you exactly who he is before you gave him more of yourself.

Interactive Assessment:

Pause here and complete the ***Your Pause Plan Assessment*** by scanning the QR code at the beginning of the book.

4

THE MYTH OF "YOU'LL LOSE HIM IF YOU DON'T"

You'll discover why setting your own pace actually increases your value and attracts the right kind of partner.

You've probably heard it before, maybe from friends, maybe from family, maybe whispered in your own head: *"If you don't give a man what he wants, he'll go find it somewhere else."* The message is blunt. If you set boundaries around physical intimacy, you'll drive him away. And in today's dating culture, where attention can evaporate with a swipe, that fear can feel real.

But let's get one thing straight: keeping your panties on does not make you "hard to get," "playing games," or "picky." It makes you clear, intentional, and in control of your most intimate gift. The pace you set isn't about withholding to manipulate; it's about protecting your clarity and making sure that access to your body is reserved for someone who has proven, through consistent action, that he's worthy of it.

If a man disappears because you won't sleep with him yet, that's not a loss; it's an instant blessing. He just showed you that his interest was transactional, and not relational. That early exit saves you months, or years, of trying to build something real with someone who was never emotionally available in the first place. He's not walking away from you; he's walking toward the next woman willing to move faster that feels right for her. And that's his pattern to carry, not yours.

The right man won't pressure you to rush. He won't question your boundaries or make you feel like your pace is a problem. In fact, a man with serious intentions will respect and even appreciate that you value yourself enough to move with purpose. Your boundaries will increase your value in his eyes, because they show you have standards, self-respect, and a vision for the kind of relationship you want.

In reality, slowing down and keeping your panties on filters faster than anything else. It reveals the men who are in it for short-term gratification and weeds them out before they can waste your emotional energy. You're not pushing anyone away; instead, you're protecting your heart, your time, and your future. The man who's worth your intimacy will be more than willing to earn it, because he's not just after your body; he's after you.

By the end of this chapter, I want you to be able to flip the script in your mind: the man who leaves because you don't move fast enough isn't "the one that got away." He's the one you never needed to begin with. And every time you choose to keep your panties on until the right man proves himself, you're not losing; you're winning.

4.1 WHERE THAT FEAR REALLY COMES FROM

The fear that you'll "lose" him if you don't move fast is rarely about the man in front of you. It's about the messages, experiences, and beliefs you've absorbed over time. It can feel real and urgent, but it's built on shaky ground. That fear often comes from:

1. **Scarcity thinking:** Believing there aren't enough good men out there, so when one shows interest, you feel pressure to do whatever it takes to keep him even if that means moving faster than you're comfortable with.
2. **Past rejection:** Remembering times when a man pulled away after you set a boundary, and assuming it will happen again. Those memories can make you equate slowing down with "scaring him off."
3. **Mixed cultural messages:** Movies, media, and even mainstream dating advice often push the idea that a woman's value lies in her ability to keep a man's attention at any cost. In those stories, a woman who "waits" is either boring or loses out to someone "more exciting."
4. **Internalized pressure:** Carrying the belief that you have to prove yourself quickly through looks, charm, or sexual availability, or you risk being replaced.

This fear is powerful because it plays on your deepest desire to be wanted, chosen, and kept. But here's the hard truth: being chosen for your body is not the same as being chosen for your worth. A man who is truly interested in you will value your boundaries and not resent them. When you keep your panties on, you're not testing his patience but his intentions. The wrong man will fail that test fast, and the right man will never make you feel like you have to buy love with your body.

4.2 HOW EMOTIONALLY MATURE MEN RESPOND TO BOUNDARIES

A man who is genuinely interested in you will not see your boundaries as an obstacle; He'll see them as a sign of strength and self-respect. He'll understand that intimacy is something earned over time, not a bargaining chip to be pressured out of you. An emotionally mature man will:

- **Respect your pace without making you feel guilty:** He won't sulk, push, or try to manipulate you into changing your mind. Instead, he'll honor your decision because he understands that trust and comfort can't be rushed.
- **Stay consistent in his effort, whether or not intimacy is on the table:** His calls, texts, and plans won't suddenly fade just because you're not moving physically as quickly as others might. His interest is steady because it's not tied to immediate gratification.
- **Value your boundaries because they reflect self-respect, not disinterest:** He knows that your willingness to protect your body and your heart shows that you take yourself seriously, and he'll admire you for it.
- **See the bigger picture:** He understands that a relationship worth having is worth building slowly, with trust and emotional safety as the foundation.

Emotionally mature men aren't scared off by boundaries, but reassured by them. They see that you have standards, that you know your worth, and that you're not willing to compromise them for short-term validation. To a man like this, keeping your panties on doesn't make you "hard to get," it makes you a woman worth keeping.

4.3 WHY LOSING THE WRONG PERSON IS A WIN

When you slow down and someone walks away, it's not rejection; it's information. That man just told you everything you needed to know without you having to waste months, or years, untangling mixed signals. He revealed that his interest was conditional, tied to how quickly he could get physical access, and not to who you are as a person. That's not a loss; it's a win. It's an early exit from a relationship that was destined to drain you.

Here's the truth most women don't hear often enough: losing someone who won't respect your pace is not proof that your standards are too high. It's proof that your boundaries are working. You are not here to convince anyone to value you. Your job is to protect your time, peace, and self-worth until someone shows they value them too.

Staying with the wrong person costs you far more than awkward dates or arguments. The price shows up in three painful ways:

- **Time you can't get back:** Months or years that could have been spent with someone aligned with your vision for love. Instead, you end up stuck in a relationship that never had a future, hoping it will turn into something it's not.
- **Emotional energy that leaves you drained**: The mental tug-of-war of trying to read between the lines, decode his behavior, and keep the relationship alive when you're the only one truly investing.
- **Self-esteem that slowly erodes**: Every time you accept being treated as an option, it chips away at your confidence and your belief in what you deserve. You start to question your worth instead of questioning his actions.

Walking away from someone who can't respect your boundaries is an act of self-protection, not self-sabotage. It's you choosing not to trade your dignity for temporary attention. It's you refusing to let someone rent space in your life when they have no intention of building anything with you.

When you keep your panties on, you fast-track this filtering process. You learn in weeks what might have taken you months to see if you'd rushed in. The man who leaves because you're not moving fast enough isn't "the one that got away." He's the one who made room for the man who will show up with patience, respect, and a genuine desire to know you. Losing the wrong person isn't just a win; it's a step closer to the relationship you actually deserve.

4.4 HOW RESTRAINT INCREASES, NOT DECREASES, YOUR VALUE

In a culture obsessed with instant gratification, restraint is rare, and rare stands out. When you keep your panties on and pace yourself, you're not playing games or being "hard to get." You're showing self-control, self-respect, and a clear understanding of your worth. That in itself sets you apart, because it sends a message that you don't hand over your time, energy, or body to just anyone who shows up with charm and attraction.

Restraint sends a clear message about how you see yourself and what you expect from a relationship. It shows:

- You're selective, not desperate. You don't say yes to every opportunity just because it's available. You evaluate whether a man is worth your intimacy before offering it.
- You're confident in real connection. You believe the right man won't vanish if you don't rush. You know that lasting relationships are built on mutual respect and shared values, not on how quickly you get physical.

- You value commitment over convenience. You're not interested in being a pit stop on someone's way to the next thrill. You're looking for something steady, and not just something exciting.

The right man will see this as a green flag. He'll recognize that you're not withholding as a power play but instead protecting something valuable. He'll respect the pace you set because he respects you, and he'll use that time to deepen the emotional connection instead of pushing for access before it's earned. If a man can't handle restraint, it's because he's not looking for a relationship that requires effort, consistency, or depth. And if he walks away because you won't move faster, he's simply proven he's not your match.

Key Insight:

If a man leaves because you set a sexual boundary, you didn't lose him; he was never yours to begin with. Boundaries don't scare away the right man; they filter out the wrong ones. Every wrong man who leaves creates space for the one who will respect your pace, your body, and your worth. Keeping your panties on doesn't reduce your value; it's one of the strongest ways to protect and preserve it.

Interactive Assessment:

Pause here and complete the ***Boundaries as a Filter Assessment*** by scanning the QR code at the beginning of the book.

5

IS HE REAL OR JUST SAYING THE RIGHT THINGS?

You'll master the skill of spotting empty words and recognizing consistent, intentional behavior.

Some men are skilled performers. They know how to say exactly what you want to hear to make you feel special, desired, and chosen. They'll tell you you're different, that they've never met anyone like you. They'll talk about vacations, shared goals, and a future together as if it's already a done deal. In those moments, it can feel like you're living inside the perfect romance.

But here's the real question: are those words a reflection of who he is, or just part of an act to get what he wants? Is he speaking from genuine intention, or is he stringing together lines he's learned that will open doors quickly, especially the bedroom door?

Many women get pulled in by those words because they feel good, and in the early rush, it's easy to focus on the fantasy instead of the facts. The problem is, words are cheap. Anyone can sound like a great partner when they're motivated by short-term attraction.

The truth about his character comes out in his behavior, especially when there's no immediate reward in sight.

This is where keeping your panties on becomes your built-in truth detector. When sex isn't on the table right away, you get to watch what happens when the "sweet talk" doesn't instantly get him what he's after. Does he keep showing up? Is his interest steady? Do his actions match the future he paints with his words? Or does his effort fade once he realizes you expect consistency before intimacy?

If a man's words are real, they'll hold up over time. If they're just a performance, the act will fall apart the moment the applause stops. And that's exactly why restraint is your advantage. It forces the mask to slip before you've invested more than he's earned.

5.1 LOVE BOMBING VS. GENUINE INTEREST

Love bombing happens when someone overwhelms you with affection, attention, and flattery early on to create a false sense of closeness. It feels intoxicating in the moment: you're getting constant texts, grand declarations, and future talk after only a handful of dates. But it's a performance, not a foundation. Once they feel they have your attention or access, the intensity fades, and so does their interest. You're left wondering how someone who came on so strong could vanish so fast.

Signs it's love bombing:

- The pace feels rushed, like you're in an emotional fast lane you didn't sign up for.
- Big promises or declarations show up before real trust has been built.

- He gets upset, sulky, or distant if you try to slow the pace or set boundaries.
- The energy and attention drop sharply once he gets what he wants, often physical intimacy.

Genuine interest looks and feels different. It moves at a steady, sustainable pace. It's not about dazzling you with grand gestures to win you over quickly but about showing you, through consistent action, that he's serious. The connection builds naturally because it's based on trust, and not adrenaline.

Signs it's genuine:

- He listens closely, remembers what you say, and follows through on what he promises.
- His interest and effort stay steady even when physical intimacy isn't part of the equation.
- He invests time in understanding you, your values, your goals, and your quirks beyond surface-level attraction.

This is where keeping your panties on becomes more than a boundary; it's a filter. Love bombing thrives on speed. Restraint forces the pace to slow, which gives you time to see if the interest is real or if it evaporates once the easy wins are gone. The man with genuine intentions won't be bothered by the pause but will use it to get closer in ways that last.

5.2 HOW CONSISTENCY EXPOSES TRUTH

Consistency is the ultimate lie detector. It's easy for a man to be charming, attentive, and "all in" for a few days or weeks when everything is new. The real test comes overtime, when the novelty wears off and there's no immediate reward. A man's true intentions are revealed not in his grand gestures at the start, but in the steady actions he takes weeks and months down the line.

Ask yourself:

- Does he keep making effort after the initial excitement? Or does his attention fade once he feels he's "got" you?
- Does he follow through on plans? Or does he cancel when something "better" or more convenient comes up?
- Is he still engaged when the pace isn't physical? Or does his interest stall when intimacy isn't on the table yet?

Consistency shows you whether his interest is rooted in you: your mind, your values, your personality, or in what he can get from you. And here's where keeping your panties on works in your favor: it extends the observation window. When sex isn't part of the early dynamic, you see whether he's invested in building a real connection or just chasing a short-term thrill.

A man with genuine intentions will keep showing up. His words and actions will match. He won't need the fast track to intimacy to stay engaged. The one who fades when the pace is slower isn't a mystery; he's your answer.

5.3 WORDS ARE EASY; WATCH WHAT HE PRIORITIZES

Anyone can say they value respect, commitment, or a serious relationship. Talking about being a "good man" or wanting "something real" is simple, and it costs nothing. The real test is in what he actually prioritizes when he has to choose between convenience and effort.

Pay attention to how he spends his time. Does he make room for you in his life consistently, or only when it fits his schedule?

Notice how he treats you when it's inconvenient for him. Does he show up when you need him, or disappear when it's not easy? Watch whether he invests in shared experiences, planning dates, outings, and moments that help you connect, or if he only suggests "hanging out" at his place. And most importantly, see if his actions match the future he talks about, because promises mean nothing without consistent and tangible steps that back them up. A man who truly values you will show it in how he allocates his time, energy, and attention. He'll prioritize actions that build the relationship, not just maintain your interest long enough to get what he wants.

This is why keeping your panties on is such a powerful filter. Without the distraction of early physical intimacy, you can clearly see what he invests in. The serious man will keep showing up, even without the instant gratification. The one who doesn't will spare you the trouble by revealing how little he prioritizes you.

5.4 TRUSTING WHAT YOU FEEL AFTER THE DATE, NOT DURING

It's easy to get swept up during a date: the chemistry, the laughter, the way he looks at you, and the little moments that make it feel like you've known each other forever. In the moment, you might feel like everything is falling into place perfectly. But that rush of excitement can blur your judgment. It's fueled by attraction, novelty, and sometimes even the desire to believe you've finally found something real. The truth is, the emotional high of a great date can be misleading if you make decisions from inside it.

The real clarity often comes after the date, once you've had time to step away from the charm, the atmosphere, and the energy of the moment. When you're no longer under that immediate emotional influence, you can think more clearly and evaluate what really happened. Ask yourself afterward: Do I feel calm, secure, and grounded, or do I feel anxious, confused, or unsettled? Did I feel genuinely heard, with space to share my thoughts and be understood, or was I just entertained and flattered? Did his actions match his words before, during, and after the date, or was there a disconnect once the evening ended?

Your post-date feelings are often a more reliable truth-teller than the buzz you feel in the moment. That's why keeping your panties on isn't just about physical boundaries but about giving yourself the breathing room to notice these emotional shifts. Without the added intensity of physical intimacy, you can trust what your gut tells you after the date instead of being swept forward by the momentum of attraction.

When you take that pause, you can see whether the connection is built on mutual respect and shared values, or if it was just a temporary high that felt good but can't sustain something lasting. A great date should leave you feeling at peace, not on edge. And if it doesn't, that's your answer.

Key Insight:

A man's words are only the preview; his actions are the full story. If you want to know if he's real, don't just listen, watch. Time and consistency will reveal everything you need to know, and keeping your panties on gives you the space to see the truth before you invest too deeply.

Interactive Assessment:

Pause here and complete the ***Actions Over Words Assessment*** by scanning the QR code at the beginning of the book.

LEAVE A REVIEW - YOUR FEEDBACK MATTERS

You've reached the halfway mark of this book.

If these chapters have helped you see relationships with clearer eyes or given you tools to protect your heart, I'd love to hear from you.

Take a minute to leave a quick review.

- Share one insight or idea that stood out to you.
- Mention how these chapters are helping you think differently about dating, boundaries, or self-respect.
- Post it on the site where you purchased the book (Amazon).

Even two or three sentences make a difference.

Your feedback helps other readers find this book and encourages women everywhere to date with confidence and clarity.

Thank you for reading, reflecting, and supporting this work.

6

SEX CAN'T SAVE A SITUATIONSHIP

You'll stop wasting energy trying to turn a dead-end connection into something real, no matter how good the chemistry feels.

If you've ever been in a situationship, you know the emotional tug-of-war it creates. You're more than friends, but not quite in a relationship. There's connection, attraction, and intimacy, but there's no clarity, no commitment, and no real forward motion. It's like being on a treadmill: you're moving, but you're not actually going anywhere.

In that in-between space, it's tempting to believe that deepening the physical side will somehow change the outcome. Maybe if you give more, he'll see what he has. Maybe if the intimacy is that good, he'll realize he doesn't want to lose you. This thinking can feel especially convincing if you've already grown attached and want to believe there's potential.

But here's the hard truth: sex can intensify what's already there, but it cannot create what's missing. If commitment isn't already on the table, physical intimacy won't magically put it there. What it will do is make it harder for you to step back when you need to, because the chemical bond created through sex will cloud your judgment and deepen your emotional attachment.

Keeping your panties on in a situationship isn't about withholding; it's about self-preservation. It gives you the clarity to see the reality without the fog of physical intimacy blurring it. If his intentions are serious, he'll work toward building something real without needing your body as proof of your value. If they're not, you'll know before you've invested even more of yourself in something that was never going to become what you wanted.

A situationship can drag on for months or years when you confuse physical closeness with emotional progress. The sooner you recognize that sex won't turn "almost" into "official," the sooner you can decide if staying in that limbo is worth your time, or if it's time to walk away.

6.1 WHY SEX WON'T CREATE COMMITMENT

Commitment is not something that just happens because two people feel good together. It's a deliberate choice. It's built on emotional readiness, shared values, and a genuine desire to build a future together. Without those three elements in place, nothing, not chemistry, not passion, not even the best sex of your life, can create lasting commitment. You can have the most electric connection, the kind that keeps you up all night talking and touching, but if his mindset isn't set on commitment, it's still just a situationship wearing the clothes of a relationship.

In fact, when you add sex to a situationship, it often locks in the lack of commitment instead of moving things forward. Here's why:

- He's already getting the benefits like closeness, companionship, emotional comfort, and physical intimacy, without having to make a single move toward defining the relationship. You're giving him relationship-level access without a relationship-level commitment.
- There's no incentive for him to step up because sex in this scenario makes it even easier for him to keep things exactly as they are. He's comfortable, you're invested, and the unspoken message is that nothing needs to change.
- The dynamic becomes harder to shift because sex creates a strong emotional bond in you through the release of oxytocin and dopamine, but it doesn't necessarily create the same shift in him. While your attachment grows deeper, his investment often stays exactly the same.

Keeping your panties on in this situation is not about punishing him or setting a trap; it's about self-protection. It's about creating space to see if his actions align with what you want before you add another layer of emotional connection that will make it harder to walk away. Sex can amplify what's already real, but it cannot manufacture commitment where it doesn't exist. The only thing it can do in a dead-end situationship is delay the moment you face the truth, and the longer you delay, the harder that truth is to accept.

The man who truly wants to build a future with you will move toward commitment without needing sex as the motivator. The man who doesn't will happily take the benefits for as long as you're willing to give them. Your boundaries, especially around intimacy, are the fastest way to find out which one you're dealing with.

6.2 HOPING IT WILL "DEEPEN" THE CONNECTION

It's easy to believe that moving things to the next physical level will automatically make the emotional bond stronger. You might tell yourself, *"Once we get closer physically, he'll feel more connected to me. He'll realize what we have is special, and he won't want to lose it."* But in most cases, what actually happens is a one-sided deepening, and it's happening in you, not in him.

Here's why:

- You feel more connected because sex triggers powerful bonding hormones like oxytocin and dopamine. These chemicals heighten feelings of attachment, trust, and emotional investment. They can make you feel like the relationship just moved forward in a meaningful way, even if nothing else has changed.
- He may enjoy the intimacy, but if he isn't mentally or emotionally ready for a committed relationship, that physical closeness won't rewrite his intentions. To him, sex can be pleasurable and even affectionate in the moment without influencing his long-term plans or making him more invested.

In other words, sex often deepens your emotional attachment while leaving his exactly where they were. That imbalance is dangerous because it creates a false sense of progress. You become more emotionally invested and more likely to overlook red flags, while he remains in the same non-committal place he was before.

Keeping your panties on gives you the breathing room to see whether his connection to you grows through the things that actually matter: shared values, consistent effort, reliability, and emotional availability. If he's not building those things without sex, it's unrealistic to expect them to appear because of it. The man who is truly committed to knowing you will deepen the relationship through his actions long before physical intimacy enters the picture. The one who isn't will reveal it just as quickly if you give yourself enough time to watch.

6.3 THE EMOTIONAL COST OF STAYING IN LIMBO

Remaining in a situationship can drain you in ways that aren't obvious at first. You might tell yourself you're "okay with it for now" because you enjoy the connection, the chemistry, and the comfort of having someone around. But under the surface, the cost builds, slowly at first, then all at once. What begins as background noise eventually seeps into deeper parts of you, wearing down the very things you need for a healthy relationship. The toll tends to show up in four main areas:

1. **Constant uncertainty:** You never truly know where you stand. One day he's attentive, the next he's distant. Every sweet moment comes with an asterisk. Does this mean something, or is it just temporary? That constant guessing keeps you on edge and robs you of the peace that comes with real security.
2. **Emotional exhaustion:** You keep showing up, investing your time, attention, and intimacy without knowing if it's building toward something real. You pour in effort hoping it will eventually pay off, but the longer it drags on without progress, the more it feels like gambling with your heart.

3. **Eroded self-esteem:** Each day he avoids defining the relationship, it chips away at your sense of worth. You start wondering if you're "enough," when in reality, the issue isn't your value, it's his unwillingness to commit. The more you accept a partial connection, the easier it becomes to believe that's all you can get.
4. **Delayed happiness:** Staying tied to someone who isn't ready for commitment means you're closed off, emotionally, mentally, and often physically, from someone who would be ready to love you fully. The right person can't step in if you're still holding space for someone who won't step up.

Every day you spend in limbo is a day you're unavailable to the kind of love you deserve. This is where keeping your panties on becomes more than a physical boundary; it's an emotional safeguard. It protects you from deepening an already unbalanced bond, and it gives you a clear vantage point to see whether the relationship is actually progressing or just keeping you stuck in place.

The truth is, limbo is still a choice. It's just a choice that works against your long-term happiness. The sooner you see you're on a treadmill, the sooner you can step off, reclaim your energy, and start moving toward a partner who is ready to meet you where you are.

6.4 BREAKING YOUR CYCLE OF OVERATTACHMENT

If you keep finding yourself stuck in situationships, it's often because you're holding on to potential instead of dealing with the reality in front of you. You tell yourself that he could commit, that he might step up, or that if you just give it more

7

STOP MISTAKING CHEMISTRY FOR COMPATIBILITY

You'll learn to tell the difference between real emotional alignment and attraction that's rooted in dysfunction.

We've all experienced it, that magnetic pull toward someone who consumes your thoughts. The spark is instant. The conversation flows effortlessly. The energy between you feels electric, almost addictive, like you've finally stumbled into the relationship you've been waiting for. In those moments, it's easy to believe that kind of attraction must mean they're "the one." The truth? Chemistry is not the same thing as compatibility.

Chemistry is a feeling. Compatibility is a fit. Chemistry is the rush in your body, the butterflies, the adrenaline, the excitement of wanting more. Compatibility is the alignment of your values, life goals, emotional readiness, and ability to work together through real-life challenges. You can have incredible chemistry with someone who is entirely wrong for you in the long term, someone who can't meet you emotionally, doesn't share your vision for the future, or has no real interest in commitment. If you keep mistaking that rush of attraction for the foundation of a lasting relationship, you'll keep chasing intensity over stability and keep ending up disappointed.

One of the biggest traps is how physical intimacy can supercharge chemistry while blurring your ability to assess compatibility. The moment you cross into sexual territory, your body releases bonding hormones like oxytocin and dopamine. These chemicals heighten attachment, making you feel more connected, more trusting, and more invested than you might actually be. You start believing the bond is deeper than it truly is, and before long, you're justifying red flags because the pull feels too strong to walk away from.

This is where keeping your panties on becomes one of your greatest tools for clarity. When you hold back physically, you give yourself the room to see if the connection holds up outside of the sexual tension. You can observe how he communicates when there's no immediate payoff, how he treats you over time, and whether he's investing in emotional intimacy as much as he's drawn to physical intimacy. Without that extra layer of chemical influence, you're free to evaluate the relationship with clear eyes rather than clouded judgment.

Real compatibility isn't built in moments of heat but in moments of consistency. It shows up in the quiet ways you support each other, the shared values that guide your decisions, and the mutual respect that makes you feel safe. The right man will give you both spark and stability, but you'll only know that for sure if you slow down long enough to see if his intentions, character, and values align with yours. Chemistry will light the fire. Compatibility will keep the fire blazing. Keeping your panties on ensures you don't confuse a flash of heat for a lasting flame.

7.1 WHY ATTRACTION FEELS SO CONVINCING

Attraction can feel so powerful that it convinces you you've found something rare and unshakable. That's because it doesn't just live in your heart but takes over your brain. When you're drawn to someone, your body releases a potent mix of dopamine, oxytocin, and adrenaline. This chemical cocktail lights up your brain like a fireworks show, making you feel euphoric, energized, and laser-focused on the other person. Under that influence, it's easy to:

- Overlook red flags because the high feels too good to question. You don't want to break the spell, so you ignore behaviors that would normally concern you.
- Confuse excitement with emotional depth, assuming that the thrill you feel means you're already deeply connected.
- Ignore incompatibilities in values, lifestyle, or long-term goals, convincing yourself those things can be "worked out later."
- Rush into physical intimacy before trust and emotional safety are established, letting the rush dictate your pace instead of your standards.

The pull of attraction can be intoxicating, but like any high, it eventually fades. When it does, the reality of who they are and how well they actually fit with you, comes into sharp focus. This is why keeping your panties on is so vital in the early stages. Without the added layer of sexual bonding hormones clouding your perception, you give yourself the space to see the whole person, not just the version your brain is infatuated with. The right man will still be there when the initial rush settles, and if he's not, you just saved yourself from investing in someone who was only there for the high.

7.2 TRAUMA BONDS DISGUISED AS "SOULMATES"

Not all powerful chemistry comes from a healthy place. Sometimes what feels like "fate" is actually a trauma bond, an intense emotional connection formed when someone's behavior triggers unresolved wounds from your past. It's not destiny pulling you together, it's familiarity. Your nervous system recognizes the pattern, even if your mind can't name it, and mistakes that familiarity for love.

Trauma bonds can be especially convincing because they feel electric and all-consuming, but that intensity is often a mix of attraction, fear, and the desperate hope for resolution. You might feel like you've met your "other half," when in reality, you've met someone who mirrors the same emotional dynamics that hurt you before.

Here are four signs your "soulmate" might actually be a trauma bond:

1. The relationship feels like an emotional rollercoaster, high highs followed by crushing lows.
2. You feel a strong need to prove yourself to them, as if earning their love will finally make you enough.
3. You confuse anxiety with excitement, mistaking the adrenaline rush of uncertainty for passion.
4. You feel drawn to them even when they hurt you, disrespect you, or make you feel unsafe.

A healthy connection won't keep you constantly on edge. It won't require you to tolerate mistreatment in exchange for occasional bursts of affection. If the bond is built on shared wounds instead of shared values, it will eventually drain you and erode your self-worth.

Keeping your panties on is one of the most effective ways to avoid falling deeper into a trauma bond. Physical intimacy in this kind of dynamic can intensify the attachment and make it even harder to walk away, no matter how badly you're being treated. By holding back, you give yourself the distance to recognize whether this "soulmate" energy is actually love or just old pain wearing a seductive mask.

7.3 DYSFUNCTION YOU'VE NORMALIZED AS PASSION

If you grew up equating chaos with love, calm can feel unsettling or even boring. When drama, volatility, or unpredictability were your "normal," stability can seem flat, even though it's the very thing you need most. The problem is, your nervous system can confuse dysfunction for passion, making healthy love feel less exciting than the rollercoaster you've been conditioned to ride.

If you've grown used to chaos in relationships, you can start to confuse unhealthy behavior with passion. Jealousy can look like love when possessiveness feels like proof someone cares. Constant arguments followed by intense makeups can feel like closeness because the relief after a fight seems exciting. Inconsistent attention can keep you chasing approval, mistaking random affection for real interest. You might even feel more attracted the more someone pulls away, believing the chase makes the love more valuable. This isn't passion, it's instability. Feeding it traps you in a cycle where the highs hook you and the lows drain you. Real love may not create adrenaline spikes, but it gives something better: steadiness, respect, and safety.

Keeping your panties on is a powerful way to interrupt this pattern. Without the chemical intensity of sex blurring your perspective, you can actually feel the difference between genuine compatibility and dysfunctional intensity. It gives you the breathing room to assess whether the connection is healthy or just familiar chaos dressed up as romance. The right relationship won't need volatility to stay alive; it will grow through consistency, not crisis.

7.4 CHOOSING PEACE OVER INTENSITY

You get to decide what you value more, the adrenaline rush of unpredictable attraction or the steady comfort of reliable love. That choice shapes the kind of relationship you build and the kind of love you allow into your life. The truth is, peace doesn't mean boring, and stability doesn't mean the spark is gone. It means you've stopped sacrificing your emotional safety for the temporary thrill of uncertainty.

Choosing peace means prioritizing how someone makes you feel when there's no performance to impress you, no dramatic moment to distract you, just the quiet, everyday spaces where the real relationship lives. It's looking for consistency over fireworks, because while fireworks are beautiful, they burn out fast. It's valuing emotional safety over constant excitement, knowing that true intimacy grows best in an environment where you feel secure. It's building connection on mutual respect, shared values, and emotional trust, not on the tension of "will he or won't he."

Chemistry still matters. It is the spark that gets the fire going, but the spark alone can't hold a relationship together. A fire without a fireplace will burn the house down. You need structure, safety, and boundaries to hold that passion in a way that warms you instead of destroys you.

This is where keeping your panties on plays a powerful role. It forces the connection to reveal itself without the shortcut of physical intimacy clouding the truth. It gives you the chance to see if a man can offer both peace and passion before you invest fully. The right man won't make you choose between excitement and security; he'll bring you both. But you can only know that for sure if you slow down and let time show you whether the attraction you feel is supported by a foundation strong enough to last.

Key Insight:

Chemistry can open the door, but compatibility is what keeps you inside. The goal isn't to give up attraction. It's about stopping attraction from blinding you to whether a person's character, values, and behavior actually align with the kind of life and love you want. When you keep your panties on, you give yourself the time and clarity to see if the spark you feel is matched by a foundation that can truly hold a relationship.

Interactive Assessment:

Pause here and complete the ***Spark or Stability? Assessment*** by scanning the QR code at the beginning of the book.

8

YOU'RE NOT "TOO MUCH"; YOU'RE JUST GIVING TOO SOON

You'll understand how over giving and overexplaining push the wrong men away, and how to reset without losing yourself.

If you've ever been told you're "too much," it's probably not because you were too loving, too caring, or too committed. It's because you gave all of that before the other person proved they'd earned it. In the early stages of dating, it's easy to fall into over-functioning. You want to make your interest clear, be supportive, and show that you're available. You believe that if you give enough of your time, effort, and attention, they'll recognize how valuable you are and respond in kind.

But giving too much, too soon doesn't create a faster path to connection. In fact, it often does the opposite. It shuts it down. When you overinvest before someone has earned that level of access, you create an imbalance. They no longer need to meet you with equal effort because you've already done the heavy lifting.

Instead of building something together, they can relax into the benefits without stepping up themselves.

This applies to emotional and physical giving. When you keep your panties on, you naturally slow the pace of how much you invest. That pause gives you the space to see if his effort matches yours without the distraction of sexual intimacy, making you feel more bonded than his actions warrant. The right man will meet your energy with his own. The wrong one will take what's offered and give as little as possible. Your job isn't to give less forever; it's to give in balance with what you receive, so you protect your time, energy, and heart for the man who's willing to earn them.

8.1 EMOTIONAL OVER-FUNCTIONING IN EARLY DATING

Emotional over-functioning is when you're doing more than your share to make the connection work. You're the one driving the relationship forward while he just goes along for the ride. It can look like you always being the one to text first or make plans, clearing your schedule to be available whenever he wants to hang out, giving him emotional support before he's actually earned your trust, and letting bad behavior slide because you want to "be understanding."

The problem is, when you're doing all the heavy lifting, you don't give him a chance to step up. You set the tone that you'll handle the work, so he doesn't have to. That might feel fine at first because you're excited and want things to go well, but over time, you'll start feeling resentful and drained. And the truth is, if someone isn't putting in effort early on, they're not suddenly going to change once they feel more comfortable.

This is why keeping your panties on matters here. It's not just about sex; it's about pacing all your giving so you can see if he's willing to match you. When you slow down and give him room to show initiative, you find out quickly whether he's serious about getting to know you or just enjoying the perks without the effort. Healthy relationships start with balanced effort from both people, not one person carrying it while the other coasts.

8.2 WHY OVER-EXPLAINING AND OVER-INVESTING BACKFIRE

Over-explaining usually comes from wanting to be understood, accepted, and seen for who you are. But in early dating, explaining yourself too much can do the opposite of what you intend. Instead of showing confidence, it can signal insecurity. It can make it seem like you're trying to talk someone into valuing you, rather than simply living your life in a way that shows your worth and letting them decide if they can meet your standards.

Over-investing too soon has a similar effect. When you give too much too quickly, your time, energy, and attention, you risk creating an unbalanced dynamic before the relationship has even formed. It can make the other person feel pressured, signal that you're available for commitment before you've even taken time to evaluate them, and set up a pattern where they contribute less because you've already taken on the majority of the effort.

Healthy attraction thrives in the space where curiosity and discovery can grow. When you keep your panties on, emotionally and physically, you give yourself that space. You allow the relationship to unfold naturally, with both people making an effort to learn about each other. That's how you find out if someone is genuinely interested in building with you, or if they were only curious until they got what they wanted.

8.3 WHAT REAL WORTHINESS LOOKS LIKE IN ACTION

Worthiness isn't something you prove; it's something you live. It's not measured by how much you give, how flexible you are, or how hard you work to be chosen. Real worthiness shows up in the quiet, consistent ways you honor yourself in dating and relationships.

It looks like matching someone's effort instead of exceeding it just to keep their attention. It's letting them pursue you without rushing to "seal the deal" or locking things down before you've truly evaluated who they are. It's understanding that your boundaries aren't obstacles but filters that naturally weed out people who aren't aligned with you. And it's knowing that the right person won't be scared off when you show self-respect; they'll lean in closer because they value those same qualities.

When you know you're worthy, you don't audition for a role in someone else's life; you decide if you want them in yours. And keeping your panties on is part of that decision-making process. It creates the time and space to see if their actions match their words, if their values align with yours, and if their interest stays steady without the shortcut of physical intimacy. That's not playing hard to get; it's living like someone who knows they're worthy of being pursued for who they are, not just for what they can give.

8.4 HOW TO RESET THE PACE WITHOUT LOSING YOURSELF

If you realize you've been giving too much too soon, you don't have to vanish, cut someone off, or start playing games to fix it. You can slow things down in a direct, respectful way that still protects your self-respect. Start by pausing the chasing. Stop being the one who always reaches out first or drives the interaction.

Give them the space to show whether they'll take initiative without you prompting them. Then, redirect your energy back into your own life, your goals, hobbies, friendships, and routines that existed before they showed up. When your life is full, you stop making them the center of it.

Next, match, not exceed, their effort. Let their actions set the baseline for what you give back. If they're making minimal effort, that's your answer, not a challenge for you to work harder. And communicate your boundaries calmly. You don't have to apologize for wanting a slower, healthier pace. Simply explain that you want to take your time and see where things go without rushing.

Resetting the pace isn't about punishing them but about protecting you. It's about ensuring the connection grows naturally, rather than being artificially sustained by your over-giving. And yes, keeping your panties on can be part of that reset. When you slow down both emotionally and physically, you can clearly see if the connection holds up when you're not carrying it. The right person will match your pace and meet you there, but the wrong one will fade, and that's information you need sooner rather than later.

Key Insight:

You're not "too much" for the right person. You're just too available for people who haven't earned that version of you yet. The right partner will take the time to get to know you, value the pace you set, respect your boundaries, and meet you with equal effort. When you keep your panties on and your energy balanced, you give the right person the chance to rise to your level, and you make it easy to spot the ones who never will.

Interactive Assessment:

Pause here and complete the ***Match Effort, Protect Energy Assessment*** by scanning the QR code at the beginning of the book.

9

RECLAIMING YOUR YES AND NO

You'll gain the confidence to set and hold boundaries without guilt, apology, or fear of losing someone.

Many women struggle to say no, especially in dating, because they fear it will push someone away, create conflict, or make them seem "difficult." So, they agree to things they don't honestly want, stay in situations longer than they should, and give parts of themselves they're not ready to give.

The truth is, every time you say yes to something that doesn't serve you, you're saying no to yourself. Over time, those choices chip away at your confidence, self-trust, and emotional energy. You end up feeling drained and undervalued, not because you're "too much," but because you've been giving too much of yourself to the wrong situations.

Reclaiming your yes and no means deciding what you want, honoring it, and refusing to shrink or bend to keep someone comfortable. The right man won't see your boundaries as a challenge or a problem; he'll see them as proof you respect yourself and expect the same in return. And when you keep your panties on until his actions prove he's earned your trust, you're not withholding but making sure your yes is intentional, and not just convenient for him.

9.1 NO IS A FULL SENTENCE

You don't owe anyone a speech, a long explanation, or a softened version of your truth just to make them comfortable. "No" is enough. It stands on its own and does not require a follow-up to be valid.

- No, I'm not ready for that yet.
- No, that doesn't work for me.
- No, I'm not interested in that kind of relationship.

When you say no with clarity and calm, you draw a clear line. A man who respects you will accept it immediately and adjust his behavior accordingly. He won't try to wear you down with charm, guilt, or persistence. He won't question your decision or make you feel like you have to justify it. If he pushes back, argues, or tries to make you second-guess yourself, he's telling you that your boundaries are inconvenient to him, which is reason enough to walk away.

The more you practice saying no without apology, the stronger your self-respect grows. You stop performing for approval and start honoring your own standards. You realize that keeping someone who needs you to bend your boundaries isn't a win; it's a slow erosion of your worth. And the men who are worth your time will never need to convince you that your no is "too much". They'll respect it the first time you say it.

9.2 BOUNDARIES THAT ATTRACT RESPECT

Boundaries aren't about shutting people out, they're about setting the tone for how you expect to be treated. They act as a filter, making it clear what's okay with you and what isn't, so there's no confusion or silent resentment later. In dating, clear boundaries communicate self-respect and give the other person the chance to rise to the standard or reveal that they can't.

Healthy dating boundaries can look like:

- Deciding how soon you're comfortable with physical intimacy and sticking to that pace.
- Being clear about how often you're available for calls, texts, or dates so you're not overextending yourself.
- Expecting respectful, consistent communication instead of tolerating disappearing acts or mixed signals.
- Holding firm to deal breakers such as dishonesty, disrespect, or controlling behavior.

The key is to enforce these boundaries consistently, not just state them. When you follow through, you naturally repel people who can't respect you and attract those who value your standards. The right man won't see your boundaries as restrictions; he'll see them as a sign that you take yourself seriously and expect the same from him.

9.3 SAYING NO WITHOUT GUILT OR OVER-EXPLAINING

If you're used to pleasing people or avoiding rejection, saying no can feel unnatural, even risky. You might worry they'll think you're cold, selfish, or difficult. To soften the blow, you may tack on long explanations, over-apologize, or try to make the "no" sound like a "maybe." The problem is that over-explaining shifts the focus from your decision to their reaction. It invites pushback, guilt trips, or attempts to negotiate you into a yes you never wanted to give.

A strong no doesn't need decorating; it needs delivery.

- **Be direct:** Use short, clear statements like "No, I'm not comfortable with that" or "No, that doesn't work for me."
- **Be calm:** Keep your tone steady. Anger makes it sound like you're defending yourself. Nervous laughter makes it sound like you don't mean it.
- **Be firm:** If they push back, repeat your no once and then change the subject or step away from the conversation.

When you learn to say no without guilt, you take back control over your time, body, and emotional bandwidth. You stop treating boundaries like invitations for debate and start treating them like the non-negotiable standards they are. And here's the thing, someone who respects you won't need three paragraphs of reasoning to accept your no. They'll hear it, honor it, and keep moving. The ones who don't? That's your sign they shouldn't have access to you in the first place.

9.4 USING SMALL BOUNDARIES TO BUILD CONFIDENCE

If setting big boundaries feels intimidating, start small. You don't have to begin by laying down an ultimatum or having a high-stakes conversation. Small boundaries give you a safe, manageable way to practice honoring your needs. They help you build confidence in your ability to speak up, follow through, and handle whatever reaction you get. Think of them as strength training for your self-respect.

These smaller boundaries might look like:

- Declining a last-minute date if it doesn't fit your schedule, instead of scrambling to rearrange your life.
- Taking your time to respond to messages, rather than feeling pressured to reply the second your phone pings.
- Saying no to an activity or favor that drains you, even if it feels minor.
- Voicing discomfort when something bothers you, rather than brushing it off to "keep the peace."

At first, you might worry about how the other person will react. But each time you set and stick to a boundary, you strengthen your trust in yourself. You prove that your needs matter, that you can protect them, and that you can survive someone's disappointment without losing yourself.

Over time, you'll notice something else: boundaries become less about defense and more about clarity. The right people won't just tolerate them but will appreciate them. And the wrong people? They'll remove themselves, which saves you from wasting your energy. Eventually, saying no when you need to, and yes when you truly mean it, will stop feeling like a risk and start feeling like the most natural thing in the world.

Key Insight:

Reclaiming your yes and no is about living in alignment with your values, priorities, and self-respect instead of bending to meet someone else's expectations. It means making choices that feel right for you, even if they disappoint or frustrate someone else. That includes keeping your panties on until you're sure a man's intentions and actions align with what you want. Saying no to sex you're not ready for, or to any level of intimacy you don't feel good about, isn't withholding, but it's protecting your time, peace, and emotional energy.

Interactive Assessment:

Pause here and complete the ***Your Yes and No Muscle Assessment*** by scanning the QR code at the beginning of the book.

10

WHAT EMOTIONALLY AVAILABLE MEN ACTUALLY DO

You'll have a clear checklist for identifying men who are ready for commitment and respect your pace.

Once you start holding your boundaries, especially when you keep your panties on until you see genuine effort and alignment, everything changes. You stop pouring yourself into men who only want access without investment. You start filtering faster, wasting less time, and noticing the ones who show up with real consistency.

The problem is, if you've spent years tangled up with men who thrive on mixed signals, hot-and-cold attention, and bare-minimum effort, real emotional availability can feel unfamiliar. When you're used to relationships that feed on anxiety and uncertainty, stability can feel almost boring at first. But that's because you've been conditioned to mistake emotional chaos for connection.

It's time to retrain your instincts. Emotionally available men do exist, and they are not subtle once you learn the signs. They don't need to be chased, decoded, or convinced to step up. They're not interested in what they can get from you as quickly as possible. They're interested in building something real, and they'll gladly match your pace, even if that means waiting for intimacy until there's trust, respect, and a shared vision for where things are going.

Keeping your panties on is more than a sexual boundary; it's a clarity tool. It allows you to see whether his interest holds steady when the instant gratification isn't on the table. An emotionally available man won't pout, pressure, or disappear because you're not rushing into bed. In fact, he'll respect you more for it, because he's not there for the short-term thrill but for the long-term connection.

Here's what these men actually do:

- They communicate openly and consistently without you having to chase them.
- They make plans in advance and follow through.
- They show genuine curiosity about your life, goals, and values; not just your body.
- They respect your boundaries, including sexual boundaries, without making it awkward or turning it into a negotiation.
- They invest time, attention, and effort into building trust before asking for more.

Once you know how to recognize these behaviors, you stop falling for the ones who only look good in the beginning. You start holding space for men whose actions match their words, who see intimacy as a natural extension of emotional connection and not as a shortcut to get there. And most importantly, you start seeing that waiting for the right person doesn't slow love down, but keeps it real from the start.

10.1 CONSISTENCY WITHOUT CONFUSION

Emotionally available men make it easy to know where you stand. They don't send mixed signals, keep you waiting by the phone, or disappear for days only to reappear when it suits them. Instead, they show steady, reliable interest from the start, and that consistency doesn't fade once they have your attention.

You'll notice it in the little things:

- They text or call regularly, without long gaps that leave you wondering if they've lost interest.
- They follow through on plans instead of canceling last minute or letting them drift into nothing.
- They show up for you in ways that aren't just about convenience or getting what they want in the moment.

When a man is genuinely emotionally available, his actions match his words consistently. He doesn't only make an effort when he's chasing you, but continues to make that effort once he has you. And here's where keeping your panties on matters. When you hold off on physical intimacy until you see this kind of reliability, you give yourself time to observe whether his consistency is real or just an act to get you into bed. A man who's truly available won't vanish, slow down, or lose interest just because you're not rushing into sex. In fact, he'll respect you more for setting that standard, and he'll value the connection you're building because it's not based solely on physical access.

If a man is inconsistent early on, believe him. That's not "him being busy" or "still figuring things out", that's his baseline. No amount of chemistry, patience, or sexual intimacy will magically make him more reliable later. Consistency is not something you should have to earn. It's something the right man offers freely, before you've given him everything, and without you having to chase it.

10.2 RESPECT FOR YOUR PACE WITHOUT PRESSURE

A man who is genuinely interested in building something real with you won't try to speed you up or wear you down. He'll respect your boundaries around both physical and emotional intimacy, and he won't make you feel like you have to "earn" his attention by giving him access to your body. Instead, he'll:

- Value the connection you're building and treat it as something worth protecting.
- Focus on getting to know you as a whole person: your thoughts, values, and daily life; not just your physical availability.
- Make you feel safe, comfortable, and in control of the pace, never rushed or pressured.

Keeping your panties on here is about more than sex; it's about seeing his intentions clearly. A man who's only in it for physical access will lose interest or push harder when he realizes you're not rushing into bed. An emotionally available man will lean into the connection without making sex the finish line.

Pressure, in any form, is a red flag. It shows a lack of respect for your boundaries and a focus on his own needs over yours. Patience is a green flag. It shows he's invested in more than just immediate gratification, and that he values the relationship you're building over the speed at which it becomes physical.

10.3 CLEAR INTENTIONS FROM THE START

An emotionally available man doesn't leave you piecing together clues about where you stand. He tells you what he's looking for and what he's ready to offer without you having to drag it out of him. If he wants a relationship, he'll say so. If he's dating with the intention of finding a partner, you'll know it from his words and his actions. He won't:

- Give you vague, "let's just see where this goes" answers when you ask what he's looking for.
- Dodge or change the subject when commitment comes up.
- Keep you in a situationship while he "figures himself out" at your expense.

Clear intentions create a foundation of trust because you know what you're signing up for. They also protect you from wasting emotional energy on someone who's just passing time. This is where keeping your panties on matters, too. When you wait to become physically intimate until you know his intentions, you're not withholding to "play games"; you're giving yourself the clarity to see if his words and actions line up. Sex can blur judgment, and an evasive man will often ride that wave to keep you invested without offering commitment. A man with clear intentions doesn't need to hide behind chemistry; he's confident about what he wants and transparent about it from day one.

10.4 MAKING YOU FEEL SAFE, NOT ANXIOUS

The easiest way to tell if a man is emotionally available is to notice how you feel when you're with him and in between seeing him. An available man doesn't just say the right things; he creates an environment where you can be yourself without fear of being judged, replaced, or strung along. With an emotionally available man, you:

- Feel secure in his interest because his actions and words align.
- Know you're respected for who you are, not just what you give.
- Can relax without constantly over-analyzing texts, tone, or timing.

With an emotionally unavailable man, you:

- Feel anxious, like you're always waiting for the other shoe to drop.
- Question if you're valued or if you're just filling a temporary space in his life.
- Feel pressure to perform, please, or prove yourself to hold his attention.

This is also where keeping your panties on works in your favor. Physical intimacy too early can trick your body into feeling bonded to someone before you've confirmed you're actually safe with them. Sex can mask red flags by releasing chemicals that make you feel closer, even if the relationship is unstable. When you protect that part of yourself until you feel true emotional safety, you give yourself time to clearly see whether he's building trust or just giving you temporary highs followed by emotional drops. If peace is your baseline with him, you're in the right place. If anxiety is your baseline, it's your sign to step back.

Key Insight:

An emotionally available man's presence is steady, calm, and consistent. You don't have to chase him down, decode mixed messages, or sacrifice your boundaries just to keep him interested. His words and actions line up, his effort is reliable, and his interest feels safe instead of stressful. He shows up because he wants to, not because you're constantly pulling him closer.

When you know what this looks like, you stop mistaking inconsistency for mystery or pressure for passion. You stop wasting months, or years, trying to turn the wrong man into the right one. Instead, you can spot emotional availability early and invest your time in someone whose presence brings clarity, peace, and respect from the start.

Interactive Assessment:

Pause here and complete the ***Spot the Green Flags Assessment*** by scanning the QR code at the beginning of the book.

11

HEALING BEFORE YOU START AGAIN

You'll release shame from past decisions, emotionally reset, and prepare yourself for healthier relationships.

You can be crystal clear on your standards, have a sharp eye for red flags, and hold firm boundaries, but if you're still carrying unhealed pain, you'll likely keep gravitating toward the same kinds of men and situations you swore you'd avoid.

Healing before you start again isn't about being perfect or waiting until you've erased every trace of your past; it's about creating enough emotional breathing room to choose differently. Without that space, you're not really starting fresh; you're just repackaging the same patterns in a new relationship.

Dating while still emotionally tied to an ex, a situationship, or heartbreak is like moving into a new house with boxes of clutter you never unpacked. You can rearrange the furniture, hang new curtains, and light a fresh candle, but eventually, the old mess spills out, taking over your new space.

When you heal first, you clear out the emotional baggage that clouds your judgment. You stop making choices from loneliness, fear, or habit, and start choosing from self-respect, peace, and genuine readiness. That's when you stop repeating history and start building something better.

11.1 HOW TO EMOTIONALLY DETOX AFTER SITUATIONSHIPS OR HEARTBREAK

An emotional detox is about clearing out the residue a person leaves behind after the connection ends: the mental and emotional scraps that keep you tied to them long after they're gone. That residue can look like:

- Obsessively replaying conversations, trying to figure out what went wrong.
- Holding on to "what if" daydreams about how it could have worked out.
- Measuring every new person against your ex, even when you know they weren't right for you.

To detox fully:

1. **Cut unnecessary contact:** Stop checking their socials, scrolling through old pictures, sending "just checking in" texts, or fishing for updates through mutual friends. Every time you peek into their life, you reopen the wound.
2. **Write it out:** Put your feelings, memories, and lessons on paper. Be honest about what happened and how it made you feel. This helps you move it out of your head and into a space where you can process and let it go.
3. **Fill your life intentionally:** The time and energy you used to give to them now need a new home. Invest it into

hobbies, friendships, personal goals, and self-care that refill your emotional reserves instead of draining them.

Detoxing isn't about erasing them from your memory. It's about reclaiming the energy, attention, and self-worth that you misplaced in that relationship so you can move forward without carrying their ghost into something new.

11.2 LETTING GO OF SHAME FROM PAST SEXUAL DECISIONS

Shame is one of the heaviest emotional weights you can carry into a new relationship. It sits quietly in the background, shaping how you see yourself and how you let others treat you. Maybe you slept with someone too soon, hoping it would bring you closer, but it only made you feel used. Maybe you stayed in a situationship far past its expiration date, telling yourself it was "better than nothing." Perhaps you overrode your own boundaries because you didn't want to lose them. Whatever it was, those choices do not define you; they were moments in time, made with the information and emotional tools you had then.

Letting go of sexual shame starts with telling yourself the truth in a new way:

- **You weren't weak.** You were human, navigating a connection the best you could.
- **You didn't "give too much."** You gave from the only place you knew how to give at the time.
- **You're not broken.** You're in the process of learning, unlearning, and evolving.

If you keep that shame locked inside, it will seep into how you date now. You might overcompensate by being hyper-vigilant, playing games, or putting on a "cool" act so you never look too eager again. Or you might shut down emotionally, keeping people at arm's length so they never get the chance to hurt you. Neither is healthy, and both rob you of the deep connection you actually want.

Here's where keeping your panties on comes in, not as a rule to punish yourself for past mistakes, but as a conscious choice to protect your emotional energy until you know someone's intentions match yours. Sex doesn't magically turn the wrong man into the right one. It doesn't guarantee commitment, respect, or emotional safety. What it can do, if you give it before trust and clarity are established, is blur your judgment and make it harder to walk away when you should.

Letting go of shame isn't about pretending the past never happened. It's about looking at those moments, extracting the lesson, and then refusing to drag the weight into your next chapter of your life. You can choose differently now, not from a place of fear, but from a place of self-respect. Keeping your panties on until you see who someone really is isn't about playing hard to get; it's about being hard to forget because you know your worth.

11.3 RESETTING YOUR SELF-IMAGE BEFORE RE-ENTERING THE DATING POOL

How you see yourself sets the tone for how others see and treat you. If you're still carrying the weight of past rejection, betrayal, or disappointment, you'll subconsciously allow people into your life who confirm that old, diminished version of you. You may tolerate less than you deserve, explain away poor treatment, or settle for "good enough" because deep down you don't believe you can have more.

Resetting your self-image begins with recognizing that your past does not define you. You are not the girl who was ghosted, cheated on, or kept in limbo; you are the woman who learned from it and now knows better. Begin to speak to yourself with the same kindness and encouragement you'd give a close friend. When old shame or doubt creeps in, replace it with proof of your progress: the boundaries you've kept, the red flags you've spotted early, the times you walked away when you once would have stayed.

Celebrate your growth instead of obsessing over your mistakes. Every choice you've made, even the ones you regret, has given you data for your future. That's wisdom you can carry forward without dragging the old pain along with it.

And yes, this also means keeping your panties on until you've seen the full picture of who someone is. Not because you're withholding, but because you've reset your standard. You're no longer proving your worth through what you give away early. You're giving yourself the gift of time, space, and clarity before you invest your body, heart, and trust. When you see yourself as a woman of value, you stop negotiating that value in relationships. The wrong men will call it "difficult." The right man will call it "exactly what I was looking for."

11.4 WHY HEALED WOMEN ATTRACT HEALTHIER PARTNERS

A healed woman doesn't walk into dating with a gaping hole she's hoping someone will fill because she is already whole. She's not searching for validation, rescue, or a quick fix to feel good about herself. She's steady, centered, and clear about what she wants, which naturally filters out people who aren't ready to meet her there.

When you've done enough healing to date from a place of peace instead of desperation, you no longer chase inconsistent people or make excuses for their lack of effort. You notice red flags early and trust yourself enough to act on them. You can enjoy the stability of a healthy partner without labeling it "boring," because you've learned that peace is far more satisfying than chaos disguised as passion.

This doesn't mean you'll never meet the wrong person again; it means you won't stay once you see they're wrong for you. Your boundaries, self-respect, and emotional clarity make it impossible to hold on to someone who can't meet your needs.

It also means you're not giving all of yourself, including your body, before you've truly seen who they are. "Keeping your panties on" is about honoring your pace and making sure physical intimacy comes with emotional safety and real commitment. Healthy, emotionally available partners respect this. They see your standards not as barriers, but as proof you value yourself, and they rise to meet that level.

Key Insight:

Before you start again, clear out the emotional baggage that keeps you tied to the past. Let go of old attachments, release shame over choices you wish you had made differently, and rebuild a self-image rooted in strength, self-respect, and clarity. Step back into dating only when your heart feels steady and your boundaries feel non-negotiable. The quality of love you attract will mirror the state you're in when you receive it, so make sure you're meeting it from a place of peace, and not pieces.

Interactive Assessment:

Pause here and complete the ***Heal, Reset, and Begin Again Assessment*** by scanning the QR code at the beginning of the book.

12

KEEPING YOUR PANTIES ON IS ABOUT POWER, NOT SHAME

You'll walk away owning your worth, protecting your peace, and dating from a position of strength, not scarcity.

Some people hear "keep your panties on" and instantly think it means you're playing games, withholding, or using sex as a bargaining chip. That's wrong. This isn't about control, manipulation, or pretending you don't want intimacy. It's about ownership of your body, your time, and your emotional energy. It's about making choices on your terms, not out of pressure, loneliness, or fear of losing someone.

Keeping your panties on means you move with intention. You decide who earns access to the most intimate parts of you, and you give that access only when their actions, consistency, and respect prove they're worth it. It's not about depriving someone. It's about protecting your peace, your clarity, and your ability to see the relationship for what it really is before sex complicates things.

It's also about breaking the cycle of letting chemistry override compatibility. You're not saying "no" forever. You're saying "not yet" until you know this person's character matches their charm. The right partner won't just tolerate that boundary; they'll respect it, because they know your self-respect means you'll also honor theirs.

12.1 THIS IS ABOUT OWNERSHIP, NOT WITHHOLDING

Withholding is a tactic. Ownership is a mindset.

- **Withholding** is about using sex as leverage to manipulate someone's behavior or emotions.
- **Ownership** is about making deliberate choices that reflect your self-respect, long-term relationship goals, and emotional safety regardless of whether someone likes it or not.

When you operate from ownership, you're not dangling intimacy like a prize to be won. You're saying, "This is my body, my heart, and my energy, and I decide when and with whom I share them." That decision isn't driven by fear of losing him or by some rule you read in a dating book. It's rooted in the awareness that sex changes dynamics. It bonds you. It deepens emotional investment. And if that bond forms before trust, clarity, and compatibility are established, it can blind you to red flags and keep you in situations you would have walked away from otherwise.

Keeping your panties on in this context is about protecting your clarity. If a man loses interest because you won't rush into sex, he's not the one you want investing your body or emotions in. The right man won't see your standards as a problem; he'll see them as a sign you value yourself, and he'll rise to meet that standard instead of trying to talk you down from it.

12.2 PROTECTING YOUR ENERGY ISN'T "BEING DIFFICULT"

Women are often branded as "difficult," "picky," or "high-maintenance" the moment they set limits or choose not to move at someone else's pace, especially when it comes to physical intimacy. But protecting your energy is not about being hard to please. It's about being intentional and discerning with who you allow into your life and into your most vulnerable spaces.

Your time, attention, emotional availability, and your body are all high-value resources. They're not an all-you-can-eat buffet for whoever shows up with a little charm and attention. They are investments that deserve careful consideration. When you give them too soon before you've had the chance to see if someone's values align with yours, if they can handle conflict maturely, if they show up consistently, and if they genuinely respect you, you risk pouring into a person who will never pour back. That imbalance doesn't just waste your time; it drains your energy, chips away at your self-respect, and leaves you feeling like you've been taken for granted.

Keeping your panties on is one of the clearest ways to protect that energy. It's about having the courage to say, "I'm not ready to share that part of myself until I know you're here for all of me, not just the parts you want access to." Sex can be beautiful, powerful, and deeply connecting, but only when it's shared with someone who has earned your trust and demonstrated their care over time.

The men who are truly worth your energy will understand and respect this. They won't pressure you, guilt you, or act like your boundaries are a problem to solve. In fact, they'll see your standards as proof that you value yourself, and that's attractive to a healthy, secure man. The ones who get irritated, pull away, or disappear the moment you set that boundary? They've just done you a favor. They've shown you they were never here for the right reasons, and now you can save your energy for someone who is.

12.3 YOU ARE NOT HARD TO LOVE; YOU'VE JUST BEEN TOO AVAILABLE TO THE WRONG PEOPLE

If you've ever been told you're too picky, too emotional, or too much work, remember that comments like that usually come from people who were never capable of meeting you where you are. It's easier for them to label you as "difficult" than to admit they can't give you the consistency, respect, or depth you deserve.

The truth is, you are not too much for the right man; you're exactly enough. The right man will see your boundaries as strength, not a burden. He'll value your standards because he values you. The problem isn't that you've been expecting too much, it's that you've been offering the best of yourself to people who were never equipped, or willing, to value it.

When you keep your panties on, you create a natural filter. It weeds out those who are only there for instant gratification and leaves space for the ones who are interested in the whole package: your mind, your heart, your values, and your life. It also forces you to slow down enough to actually see if a man's words match his actions, if his intentions are real, and if his behavior holds up over time.

12.4 SELF-RESPECT IS YOUR STRONGEST FILTER

At the end of the day, self-respect protects you more than any dating tip, rule, or checklist ever could. When you have it, you don't need to keep second-guessing someone's intentions. You simply watch how they show up and act accordingly. When you respect yourself:

- You don't bend your boundaries to keep someone interested.
- You don't mistake attention for genuine affection or commitment.
- You leave situations that chip away at your peace, even if walking away is hard.

Self-respect works like an internal sorting system. It doesn't stop you from meeting the wrong people; it just makes sure you don't stick around trying to convince them to be right for you. It cuts down the emotional noise so you can see clearly who's showing up with honesty, consistency, and care.

And here's the truth: when your self-respect is high, you don't have to "test" anyone. You don't have to overthink how long to wait before being intimate or fear you'll scare someone off by keeping your panties on. The wrong men will disqualify themselves quickly, and the right man will see your standards as proof that you know your worth. Dating gets easier when you stop making it about keeping someone and start making it about keeping yourself.

Key Insight:

Keeping your panties on isn't about shame; it's about power. It's about saying, "I decide who gets access to me, and I decide it on my terms." It's the recognition that your time, your body, and your heart are not open for casual withdrawal. They are privileges earned through consistency, respect, and genuine connection.

You are the prize not because you're playing hard to get, but because you are hard to earn. You've learned how to slow down and watch how a man shows up over time. You've learned to protect your boundaries, to stop confusing attention for affection, and to stop giving the best of yourself to men who haven't proven they can handle it. You've taken the time to heal from the past, so you're not repeating it.

Now, the rest is in your hands. You don't have to prove your worth, over-give, or lower your standards to keep someone interested. You only have to act like you know your value and trust that the right man will meet you there. And when that man comes, you won't feel anxious, rushed, or unsure. You'll feel steady. Safe. Seen. You won't have to guess if it's real because his actions will make it obvious.

Interactive Assessment:

Pause here and complete the ***Power, Not Shame Assessment*** by scanning the QR code at the beginning of the book.

CONCLUSION: YOUR POWER, YOUR PACE, YOUR CHOICE

You've just walked through twelve chapters that challenged the way you think about dating, intimacy, and your own worth. Along the way, you've learned that keeping your panties on has nothing to do with playing games or following outdated rules. It's about owning your body, your time, and your emotional energy.

You now know:

- **Sex isn't a shortcut to love:** It can create an illusion of connection, but it doesn't replace trust, time, and shared values.
- **Rushing hides red flags:** Slowing down reveals who someone truly is.
- **Boundaries don't push away the right man:** They filter out the wrong ones.
- **Chemistry is not compatibility:** Peace and consistency are just as important as attraction.
- **Over-giving too soon costs you:** Healthy love is built when effort is mutual.

- **Emotionally available men show up differently:** You can now spot the signs.
- **Healing before you start again changes everything:** A whole, confident woman chooses better because she knows she's worth more.

At the heart of all of this is one truth: you are not too much, too picky, or too hard to love. You've simply been too available to men who weren't capable of giving you what you deserve. That ends now.

Keeping your panties on is not about depriving anyone but about protecting yourself long enough to see if the person in front of you has the patience, integrity, and consistency to be worth your "yes." It's about dating from a place of self-respect instead of fear.

From here forward, you have a choice every time you meet someone new:

- You can go back to the old patterns: rushing in, hoping for the best, and ignoring what you've learned.
- Or you can date with clarity, confidence, and the courage to walk away from anything that doesn't feel right.

The right man will never need to be convinced of your value. He will recognize it, respect it, and match it. And when that man shows up, you won't hesitate to take off your panties and give them to him, gladly, freely, and without a single doubt because by then, you'll know he's earned it.

You hold the power now. Your pace sets the tone. Your boundaries shape the outcome. And your self-respect will always be the strongest filter you have. From this point on, remember: you don't have to prove your worth to anyone; you just have to live like you know it.

YOUR REVIEW HELPS OTHER WOMEN FIND THIS BOOK

Thank you for reading to the end.

If this book helped you protect your heart, strengthen your boundaries, or date with more confidence, please take a few moments to share your thoughts.

Leave a quick review where you purchased the book.

- Write a few sentences about the most valuable lesson or insight you're taking away.
- Mention how the book has influenced your perspective on dating, self-respect, or emotional clarity.
- Post it on Amazon **[link to amazon]**

Your feedback not only supports this work but also helps other readers discover a resource that may change the way they see relationships.

Every short review makes a difference. Thank you for adding your voice.

Assessments and Worksheets:

Assessments & Worksheets (Free Download)

REFERENCES

Acevedo, B. P., & Aron, A. (2014). Romantic love, pair-bonding, and the brain: An overview. *Oxford handbook of close relationships* (pp. 3–36). Oxford University Press.

American Psychological Association. (2008, February). The two faces of oxytocin. *Monitor on Psychology.*

Aron, A., & Aron, E. N. (2018). *Love and the expansion of self: Understanding attraction and satisfaction.* Routledge.

Baumeister, R. F., & Vohs, K. D. (2004). Sexual economics: Sex as female resource for social exchange in heterosexual interactions. *Personality and Social Psychology Review, 8*(4), 339–363.

Birnbaum, G. E., & Finkel, E. J. (2015). The magnetism that holds us together: Sexuality and relationship maintenance across relationship development. *Current Opinion in Psychology, 1,* 29–33.

Birnbaum, G. E., & Reis, H. T. (2019). Eager to connect, reluctant to commit: Avoidant attachment predicts rapid sexual involvement in romantic relationships. *Personality and Social Psychology Bulletin, 45*(4), 540–553.

Brewer, G., Hunt, D., James, G., & Abell, L. (2018). Dark triad traits, infidelity and romantic relationship dissolution. *Personality and Individual Differences, 135,* 1–6.

Brown, B. (2010). *The gifts of imperfection: Let go of who you think you're supposed to be and embrace who you are.* Hazelden Publishing.

Brown, B. (2012). *Daring greatly: How the courage to be vulnerable transforms the way we live, love, parent, and lead.* Gotham Books.

Brown, B. (2015). *Rising strong: How the ability to reset transforms the way we live, love, parent, and lead.* Spiegel & Grau.

Brown, B. (2018). *Dare to lead: Brave work. Tough conversations. Whole hearts.* Random House.

Buss, D. M. (2016). *The evolution of desire: Strategies of human mating* (4th ed.). Basic Books.

Campbell, L., & Stanton, S. C. E. (2019). Adult attachment and trust in romantic relationships. *Current Opinion in Psychology, 25,* 148–151.

Carnelley, K. B., & Rowe, A. C. (2010). Repeated priming of attachment security influences later views of self and relationships. *Personal Relationships, 17*(1), 37–56.

Carter, C. S. (2003). Oxytocin and sexual behavior. *Neuroscience and Biobehavioral Reviews, 16*(2), 131–144. https://doi.org/10.1016/S0149-7634(02)00045-9

Cloud, H., & Townsend, J. (2000). *Boundaries in dating: How healthy choices grow healthy relationships*. Zondervan.

Cloud, H., & Townsend, J. (2017). *Boundaries: When to say yes, how to say no to take control of your life* (Updated and expanded ed.). Zondervan.

Dodds, S., & Thomson, C. (2021). Sexual consent, autonomy, and the ethics of sexual activity. *Journal of Applied Philosophy, 38*(2), 185–200.

Eastwick, P. W., & Finkel, E. J. (2008). Speed-dating and romantic desirability: Who is desirable and why? *Personality and Social Psychology Bulletin, 34*(12), 1667–1679.

Eastwick, P. W., & Finkel, E. J. (2008). Sex differences in mate preferences revisited: Do people know what they initially desire in a romantic partner? *Journal of Personality and Social Psychology, 94*(2), 245–264.

Estlein, R., & Weinstein, N. (2021). Self-respect, authenticity, and autonomy: The role of self-respect in psychological well-being. *Journal of Happiness Studies, 22*(5), 2217–2237.

Feuerman, M. (2017). *Am I normal if?: And other questions you might ask your therapist*. St. Martin's Griffin.

Fine, E., & Schneider, S. (1995). *The rules: Time tested secrets for capturing the heart of Mr. Right*. Warner Books.

Fisher, H. E., & Brown, L. L. (2018). Lust, attraction, and attachment in mammalian reproduction. *Hormones and Behavior, 98*, 45–53.

Fisher, H. E., Aron, A., & Brown, L. L. (2006). Romantic love: A mammalian brain system for mate choice. *Philosophical Transactions of the Royal Society B: Biological Sciences, 361*(1476), 2173–2186.

Ginter, A. (2024, October 14). How to set physical boundaries when dating. *Boundless*.

Grewen, K. M., Girdler, S. S., Amico, J. A., & Light, K. C. (2005). Effects of partner support on resting oxytocin, cortisol, norepinephrine, and blood pressure before and after warm partner contact. *Psychosomatic Medicine, 67*(4), 531–538.

Hall, J. H., & Fincham, F. D. (2008). Relationship dissolution following infidelity: The roles of attributions and forgiveness. *Journal of Social and Clinical Psychology, 27*(5), 479–504.

Hall, S. S. (2019). Delaying sexual involvement and relationship outcomes: The protective role of pacing. *Archives of Sexual Behavior, 48*(2), 505–518.

Hammond, M. D., Overall, N. C., & Cross, E. J. (2016). When relationships grow: The role of relationship-specific incentives and motives in relationship maintenance. *Journal of Personality and Social Psychology, 110*(5), 709–729.

Harris, J. (1997). *I kissed dating goodbye*. Multnomah Books.

Johnson, S. M. (2019). *Attachment theory in practice: Emotionally focused therapy (EFT) with individuals, couples, and families*. Guilford Press.

Jonason, P. K., Li, N. P., & Buss, D. M. (2010). The costs and benefits of the Dark Triad: Implications for mate poaching and mate retention tactics. *Personality and Individual Differences, 48*(4), 373–378.

Kiang, L., & Buchanan, C. M. (2014). Daily stress and emotional well-being during adolescence: The moderating role of parental warmth. *Journal of Marriage and Family, 76*(5), 1039–1054.

Knapp, J. E., & Taylor, J. M. (2020). Friends with benefits relationships: Understanding motivations and outcomes. *Journal of Sex Research, 57*(2), 192–204.

Lawson, D. M., & Brossart, D. F. (2013). Interpersonal interaction patterns of women in relationships with narcissistic men. *Journal of Counseling & Development, 91*(3), 293–300.

Lerner, H. G. (2017). *The dance of connection: How to talk to someone when you're mad, hurt, scared, frustrated, insulted, betrayed, or desperate*. Harper Paperbacks.

Levine, A., & Heller, R. (2010). *Attached: The new science of adult attachment and how it can help you find—and keep—love*.

Mark, K. P., & Herbenick, D. (2014). The impact of emotional intimacy on sexual satisfaction in heterosexual relationships. *Journal of Sex & Marital Therapy, 40*(3), 198–215.

Mark, K. P., Garcia, J. R., & Fisher, H. E. (2015). Perceived emotional and sexual satisfaction across sexual relationship contexts: Friends with benefits, romantic partners, and casual encounters. *Journal of Sex Research, 52*(6), 688–698.

Markman, H. J., Stanley, S. M., & Blumberg, S. L. (2010). *Fighting for your marriage: Positive steps for preventing divorce and preserving a lasting love* (3rd ed.). Jossey-Bass.

Mikulincer, M., & Shaver, P. R. (2016). *Attachment in adulthood: Structure, dynamics, and change* (2nd ed.). Guilford Press.

Neff, K. (2011). *Self-compassion: The proven power of being kind to yourself*. William Morrow.

Pennebaker, J. W., & Smyth, J. M. (2016). *Opening up by writing it down: How expressive writing improves health and eases emotional pain* (3rd ed.). Guilford Press.

Perel, E. (2017). *The state of affairs: Rethinking infidelity*. Harper.

Pincus, J. D., & Ansell, E. B. (2013). Interpersonal theory of personality. In T. A. Widiger (Ed.), *The Oxford handbook of personality disorders* (pp. 75–99). Oxford University Press.

Rusbult, C. E., Olsen, N. O., Davis, J. L., & Harmon, P. A. (2001). *Close romantic relationships: Maintenance and enhancement*. Psychology Press.

Simpson, J. A., & Rholes, W. S. (2017). Adult attachment, stress, and romantic relationships. *Current Opinion in Psychology, 13,* 19–24.

Smith, T. W., Uchino, B. N., Berg, C. A., Florsheim, P., Pearce, G., & Hawkins, M. (2012). Affiliation and control in marital interaction: Metaphors for marital relationships. *Journal of Family Psychology, 26*(2), 153–164.

Sternberg, R. J. (1987). Liking versus loving. *Psychological Bulletin, 101*(3), 417–432. https://doi.org/10.1037/0033-2909.101.3.417

Tatkin, S. (2016). *Wired for dating: How understanding neurobiology and attachment style can help you find your ideal mate.* New Harbinger.

Tashiro, T., & Frazier, P. (2003). "I'll never be in a relationship like that again": Personal growth following romantic relationship breakups. *Personal Relationships, 10*(1), 113–128.

Timm, T. M., & Keiley, M. K. (2011). The effects of differentiation of self, adult attachment, and sexual communication on sexual and marital satisfaction: A path analysis. *Journal of Sex & Marital Therapy, 37*(3), 206–223.

Van Epp, J. (2007). *How to avoid falling in love with a jerk: The foolproof way to follow your heart without losing your mind.* McGraw-Hill.

ALSO BY DR. A.M. BENJAMIN:

In *The EQ of Dating,* Dr. Benjamin guides you through the most powerful skill you'll ever need in dating: emotional clarity. This isn't about how to get someone to like you —it's about how to stop losing yourself in emotionally unavailable dynamics and start building meaningful, secure relationships from the inside out.

Whether you're newly single, in your 20s or your 60s, healing from heartbreak, or ready to raise your standards in love, *The EQ of Dating* is your roadmap to connection that doesn't drain, confuse, or leave you questioning your worth.

The 5 Connection Styles: Why Emotional Intelligence is the New Love Language shows you how to move beyond scripted gestures and create a connection that feels alive, mutual, and safe. Dr. A.M. Benjamin reframes the classic five love languages into five EQ-driven connection styles: Verbal, Action, Giving, Time, and Contact.

Written from a father's perspective to his strong and successful adult daughter, this book is meant to be her guide and it can be yours too.

Backed by research and shaped by the author's own journey of transformation, this book is about *lasting change*. You'll develop the mindset and habits that top performers and emotionally intelligent leaders rely on to thrive in fast-paced, high-stakes environments.

Whether you're managing teams, navigating relationships, or seeking personal growth, *Emotional Intelligence for the Busy Professional* is your essential companion. In just 30 days, you'll not only understand emotional intelligence—you'll lead with it, live by it, and see the difference in every interaction.

This book empowers teens with the knowledge and skills to navigate personal finance confidently. From budgeting and saving to investing and building wealth, teens will gain the tools they need to take control of their financial future — and avoid common pitfalls.

With expert advice and practical strategies, parents can rest assured knowing their teens are on the path to financial independence before adulthood. Don't let your teen face the financial world unprepared. Start building their financial foundation today!

ABOUT THE AUTHOR

Dr. A.M. Benjamin has dedicated his career to leadership and management across federal, state, and local government sectors. With over 12 years of experience teaching at the graduate level, he is passionate about equipping teens and young adults with the skills they need for lifelong success. Dr. Benjamin empowers young people and working professionals alike to build strong money, people, and management skills.

CONNECT WITH DR. A.M. BENJAMIN

www.ingramcontent.com/pod-product-compliance
Ingram Content Group UK Ltd.
Pitfield, Milton Keynes, MK11 3LW, UK
UKHW021919190726
13853UKWH00002B/749

9 798994 522165